ELEMENTARY PRINCIPLES OF CHRIST

"Now let us move on to perfection, not laying again the foundation of repentance..." Hebrews 6:1

Laying a Solid Christian Foundation to attain Spiritual Maturity

Tunde K. Thompson-Oritogun

Elementary Principles of Christ
Copyright (c) 2008 by Tunde Thompson-Oritogun
Revised 2023

Published by
Sophos Books
163 Warbank Crescent
Croydon
CR0 0AZ

On behalf of
Manna Mercy Ministries International

The scripture quotations in this publication are from the NEW KING JAMES VERSION copyright 1979, 1980, 1982, 1991 by Thomas Nelson, Inc.

ISBN 978-1-905669-38-7

All rights reserved. No part of this publication may be reproduced, stored in a retrieval system, or transmitted in any form or by any means, electronic, mechanical, photocopy, recording or any other, without the prior permission of the author.

Cover design by Tope Enoch

Printed in the United Kingdom

TABLE OF CONTENTS

Dedication — 5

Introduction — 7

Prayers For The Readers — 11

Chapter 1
Dynamics Of The Kingdom Of God — 13

Chapter 2
Understanding The Dynamics Of Salvation — 25

Chapter 3
Dynamics Of The Word Of God — 65

Chapter 4
Understanding The Importance Of The Elementary Principles Of Christ — 81

Chapter 5
Foundation Of Repentance From Dead Works — 95

Chapter 6
Faith Towards God — 113

Chapter 7
Doctrines Of Baptism — 125

Chapter 8
The Laying On Of Hands — 143

Chapter 9
Resurrection Of The Dead — 149

Chapter 10
Eternal Judgment And Rewards — 157

Chapter 11
Full Assurance Of Salvation For New Believers — 175

Chapter 12
Daily Prayers For New Believers — 189

Word Search - The Word of God — 197

Word Search - Elementary Principles Of Christ — 199

Bibliography — 201

Prayer Of Salvation — 202

DEDICATION

I dedicate this work to God and our savior Jesus Christ for the gift of salvation and the gift of teaching His word (an earthen vessel created for the Master's use) and for the grace to walk closely with the Father, Son and Holy Spirit. and the great treasure given to me.

To my teacher; the Holy Spirit, for giving me a heart to learn from Him; for His guidance, direction and leading. For the Spirit of wisdom, knowledge and understanding that has enabled me to write this training manual and workbook for prayer.

To all christian spiritual leaders who love Jesus, His Second Coming and the Bride of Jesus; and all believers who desire to see new believers have a solid biblical foundation and grow into spiritual maturity.

INTRODUCTION

You are welcome into the household of God; the most powerful, glorious, triumphant, blessed, victorious, indestructible, undefeated, everlasting, and greatest family on earth.

Being born again is a spiritual re-birth, it transcends any natural experience. Now that you are born again, you have been birthed into a new kingdom – the Kingdom of God. There are 3 specific kingdoms known to man – kingdom of this world (earthly); kingdom of Satan (spiritual) and kingdom of God (spiritual). Jesus said that you are in this world but not of this world.

> *"They are not of the world, even as I am not of it"* -
> **John 17:16.**

As with every kingdom, there are rules, regulations, and laws (precepts and statutes) that govern the Kingdom of God which every citizen must understand and obey fully in order to live a life of victory. Just as the laws in

England are not applicable in Bulgaria; so also, the laws in the earthly kingdom are in opposition to the laws in the kingdom of God. In the light of this understanding, every child of God must have a solid foundation of some basic laws in the Kingdom of God in order to attain spiritual maturity, take hold of the promises of God and live victorious lives.

In this book, we will explore the following topics:

- Understanding Salvation and its blessings, the message of the kingdom, the reasons Jesus came to the earth, was crucified, buried and his resurrection.
- Understanding the Holy Spirit – the Spirit of God.
- Understanding the role of the Holy Spirit as our helper, guide, teacher, counsellor, comforter, and gift giver.
- Understanding the elementary principles of Christ (Repentance from dead works, faith in God, doctrines of baptism, resurrection, and eternal judgement).
- Understanding the assurance of salvation that enables new believers stand firm in times of spiritual weakness, trials, testing and persecution from unsaved relatives, friends, and satanic agents.
- The availability of graces to attain perfection (maturity).

Finally, powerful, and practical biblical prayer points have been made available for daily prayers to help give you spiritual strength, wisdom from God, a revelation of your purpose on earth to achieve your spiritual goals and eventually receive your crown of righteousness and reign with Him forever in heaven! To achieve all of this, you must have a solid foundation.

What is a Foundation? In the natural sense, it is a solid ground or base on which a building rests or a body or ground on which other parts are overlaid. In the spiritual sense, a foundation is the underlying principles governing a church or an organization. For you as a believer, it is the life principles God has made available in His word on which you should build your Christian life. The word of God declares in Psalm 11:3 "if the foundation be destroyed what can the righteous do" and in "I Corinthians 3:10-13, it says, "For no other foundation can anyone lay than that which is laid which is Jesus Christ. In other words, building a foundation on the knowledge of God's word is the key to spiritual growth and maturity and knowledge can only be gotten by memorizing, meditating, and confessing the word every day.

A solid foundation in the word of God will also help you avoid the landmines Satan sets for every believer to cause them to stumble and fall. The devil tried to stop you from getting saved, but he has failed, but he will keep trying. He will stop at nothing to kill, steal and destroy the destiny of a believer; if you do not have a solid foundation in God's word and principles, you will fall prey of his plans. His ultimate goal is to make you doubt the unconditional love God has for you, make you feel defeated and then backslide. Be encouraged that Jesus prayed for you, to make it to heaven; He said "Father, I desire that they also whom You gave Me may be with me where I am, that they may behold My Glory which you have given me; for You loved me before the foundation of the world" John 17:24

My prayer for you is that you will grasp and apply the principles in this book to your life and live a life of victory in Christ Jesus.

PRAYER FOR THE READERS

Dear Heavenly Father, in the name of Jesus, I thank you for the lives of my brothers and sisters reading this book, thank you for the salvation of their souls, thank you for the baptism of the Holy Spirit and fire. I thank you for the call of God upon their lives and I thank you for the spirit of wisdom, revelation, and discernment you are imparting to them now as they read. I also thank you because I know you will take them to a new level of spiritual growth and maturity.

Now I pray that the Lord who began a good work in you will faithfully complete it to the end. May you discover the Lord's purpose for your life (the unique, specific, and individual divine assignment) and may you receive all the tools necessary to fulfill this assignment (spiritual, material, financial resources, and human help) to the last detail. May the Lord grant you grace to run the race set before you with joy. May the Lord keep you strong to the end and keep you blameless on the day of our Lord Jesus Christ. May you persevere under trial, withstand every test and receive the crown of life promised to all who love Jesus.

Now may the God of peace Himself sanctify you completely, preserve your spirit, soul, and body until the coming of our Lord JESUS. Finally, may the God of peace, equip you with everything good to do His will, and may He work in you what is pleasing to Him, through Jesus Christ, to whom be glory for ever and ever. Amen.

CHAPTER 1

DYNAMICS OF THE KINGDOM OF GOD

AIM:
To enable believers to understand the dynamics of God's kingdom.

OBJECTIVES:
At the end of the teaching, believers should be able to:
- Have a better understanding of the characteristics of God's kingdom.
- Explain the authority, blessings and responsibilities of being part of God's kingdom.

SECTION A
UNDERSTANDING THE KINGDOM OF GOD

What is a Kingdom?
A kingdom is an organized community headed by a king or queen with all its territories subject to him/her.

It is quite evident that there are 3 different types of Kingdoms known to man, namely: EARTHLY KINGDOM, SATANIC KINGDOM & GOD'S KINGDOM.

For the purpose of this teaching, we shall be dealing with the kingdom of God.

THE KINGDOM OF GOD

What is the Kingdom of God?
The Bible gives us this definition:

> *"The Kingdom of God is Righteousness (just, UPRIGHTNESS and right standing with God), Peace and Joy in the Holy Spirit.* – **Romans 14:17**

The scriptures further affirm that, *"He has delivered us from the power of darkness and conveyed us (transferred us) into the Kingdom of the Son of His Love* – **Colossians 1:13**

"In **Luke 22:29 Jesus said** *"And I confer unto you a kingdom, just as my Father conferred one on me…"*

This kingdom is ruled by **Jesus** who is the King of all Kings and the Lord of Lords. HE IS THE HEAD OF THE KINGDOM OF GOD and all authority has been given to Him by God. Matthew 28:18 says; *And Jesus came to them and said all authority in heaven and on earth has been given to me"* and He will rule in partnership with believers who He has made kings and priests *"and have made us Kings and Priests to our God; and we shall reign on earth* - Revelation 5:10. Together, we will rule with Jesus and have dominion on the earth now and in ages to come.

In the next section, we will examine the characteristics of God's kingdom.

SECTION B

The Characteristics of God's Kingdom

The characteristics of God's kingdom are complete expressions of its quality, power, uniqueness, and greatness. We will examine all these characteristics as they are described in the bible.

1. **Repentance** opens the gate into the kingdom; the scripture says: *"Repent for the kingdom of God is at hand"* (it is here, it is in operation here on earth) – **Matthew 4:17.**

2. **"The Kingdom of God is within you"**. Every believer carries the kingdom of God; we are ambassadors of God's kingdom and represent Him everywhere we go. We are to dominate every sphere of life and subdue the power of satan so that God's kingdom can be established on earth. *Jesus replied, "The Kingdom of God does not come with your careful observation, nor will people say, "here it is, or there it is, because the kingdom of God is within you".* – **Luke 17:20b – 21.**

3. You must be **born again** to **see** or **enter** the Kingdom of God. It is the only way the Lord made available to have access to His kingdom.

    In reply Jesus declared, "I tell you the truth, no one can see the kingdom of God unless he is born again" – **John 3:3**

    Jesus answered, "I tell you the truth, no one can enter the kingdom of God unless he is born of water and the Spirit – **John 3:5**

4. Jesus has given every believer **The Key** of the kingdom to subdue the activities of satan on earth (it locks and opens doors on earth and in the heavenly places).

> *"Behold, I give you the authority to trample on serpents and scorpions, and over all the power of the enemy and nothing shall by any means hurt you."* – **Luke 10:19.**

5. The Kingdom of God is **not of this world** (it is a spiritual Kingdom and its origin is not natural, it is not of the secular world system, nor of the world order; hence it is not of this world, yet has all the resources and power to manifest in this world) *Jesus answered, "My kingdom is not of this world. If My kingdom were of this world, My servants would fight, so that I should not be delivered to the Jews; but now My kingdom is not from here."* - **John 18:36.**

6. The Kingdom of God is **not in word but in power** (it has the resources to demonstrate the power of the Holy Spirit, to declare the name of Jesus and destroy the works of satan) – **I Corinthians 4:20.**

7. The Kingdom of God is **righteousness, peace and joy in the Holy Spirit** (in this Kingdom, there is divine empowerment to live a righteousness, holy, joyful and peaceful lifestyle through Christ Jesus. – **Romans 14:17.**

8. Believers are **translated** from the Kingdom of darkness into the Kingdom of God (through the process of Salvation)

> *"He has delivered us from the power of darkness and conveyed us into the Kingdom of the Son of His love"*
> – **Colossians 1:13.**

9. It is an **everlasting** kingdom (it is not temporary, it has no beginning, it has no end, it will endure forever and ever) *"Your kingdom is an everlasting Kingdom, and Your dominion endures throughout all generations"* – **Psalm 145:13.**

10. The Kingdom of God is **a priority** for everyone. Seeking the kingdom of God is the key to release other blessings and revelations. Jesus admonished every believer to: *"...seek his kingdom and His righteousness, and all these things will be given to you as well"* - **Matthews 6:33.**

11. The **MYSTERIES** of the kingdom is revealed to the believers, not to unbelievers - a **Mystery** means something hidden – secrets, hidden spiritual truths that can only be revealed through revelation from the Holy Spirit; - an unregenerated human spirit cannot understand it. *"The mystery that had been kept hidden for ages and generations but is being disclosed to the saints. To them God has chosen to make known among the Gentiles the glorious riches of this mystery, Christ in you, the hope of glory".-* **Colossians 1:26.**

12. This mystery is the word of God in its fullness, the message of the cross and all the attributes of the character of Jesus Christ being made manifest in the believer. Jesus further affirmed that *"the knowledge of the secrets of the Kingdom of heaven has been given to you, but not to them"* - **Matthew 13:11.**

13. The **SCEPTRE** (ruling staff of authority) of God's kingdom is **righteousness – Hebrews 1:7** When you are made righteous through the cleansing of our sins by the redemptive blood of Jesus, you receive the right to use the scepter of the kingdom. **(2nd Corinthians 5:21);** The scepter gives you power, authority and dominion over the devil and anything that opposes the purposes of God on earth.

Righteousness also serves as a weapon against satan and his spiritual host of wickedness. *"And do not present your members (parts of your body) as instruments (weapons) of unrighteousness to sin, but present your yourselves to God as being alive from the dead, and your members as instruments of righteousness to God"* –**Romans 6:13.**

14. It is a kingdom that **cannot be shaken** - This kingdom has ability to withstand the assault of the devil and hold back all the activities of satan on earth. *"Therefore, since we are receiving a kingdom which cannot be shaken, let us have grace, by which we may serve God acceptably with reverence and godly fear"* - **Hebrews 12:28**.

15. The **greatest virtue** in God's kingdom is **Humility**. The word of God declares that: *"therefore whoever humbles himself as this little child is the greatest in the kingdom of heaven* – **Matthew 18:4**.
(Virtue means moral excellence; uprightness; goodness; good quality in a person). *Therefore, humble yourself as Jesus did and set an example for us to follow. "Let this mind be in you which was also in Christ Jesus, who being in the form of God, did not consider it robbery to be equal with God, but made Himself of no reputation, taking the form of a bondservant and coming in the likeness of men. And being found in the appearance as a man. He humbled Himself and became obedient to the point of death, even the death on the Cross. Therefore God also has highly exalted Him and given Him the name which is above every name, that at the name of Jesus every knee should bow..."* - **Philippians 2:5-11**.

16. The **greatest sin** of the kingdom is **Pride** (the proud cannot live successfully in this kingdom because God opposes the proud and gives grace to the humble)

> *"And whoever exalts himself will be humbled (put down) , and he who humbles himself will be exalted (lifted up) "*– ***Matthew 23:12***

17. The **Citizens** of the kingdom are **Believers.**

> *"For our citizenship is in heaven, from which we also eagerly wait for the Savior the Lord Jesus "*
> – **Philippians 3:20**

18. The **Currency** of the kingdom is the name of **Jesus** (by faith, His name has paid the price for all things – healing from diseases & sickness, poverty, lack, death, curses & deliverance from all addictions). *"Silver and gold I do not have… in the name of Jesus Christ of Nazareth, rise up and walk"* –**Acts 3:6**.

19. The **Ambassadors** of the kingdom are the **Disciples** of Jesus (**Believers**) and anyone who accepts Him as Lord and Saviour are appointed by Him to represent God on earth – *"Now we are ambassadors for Christ, as though God were pleading through us …"*
 - 2 Corinthians 5:20.

20. The **Message of the kingdom** is foolishness to unbelievers, but to believers it is the **power of God.** The product of this message is **salvation of souls** – *"For the message of the Cross is foolishness to those who are perishing, but to us, who are being saved, it is the power of God"*
 - I Corinthians 1:18.

21. The **Greatest person in the kingdom is the one who serves** others (servant hood) *"but he who is greatest among you shall be your servant"*
 - **Matthew 23:11.**

22. **The person who teaches and practices the word of God** will be called **GREAT** in the kingdom of God.

> *"Whoever therefore breaks one of the least of these commandments, and teaches men so, shall be called least in the kingdom of heaven; but whoever does and teaches them, he shall be called **great in the kingdom of heaven"* – **Matthew 5:19.**

QUESTIONS

1. What do you understand by the term *My kingdom is not of this world?* As a citizen of God's kingdom, how do you live your life here on earth without being polluted by the world system? (Read John 17:14).

2. The Lord instructed us to *"Seek first the Kingdom of God and His righteousness"* Do you find it easy or difficult to place the priorities (salvation of souls, serving the Lord and propagating the gospel of Jesus e.t.c.) of the Kingdom of God above your own priorities (i.e. food, clothing, material things and money)? If you find it challenging, what steps can you take to obey the divine instructions of the Lord?

3. *"The mystery that had been kept hidden for ages and generations"*. What is this mystery of the kingdom?

4. Explain in your own words your understanding of this term "Christ in you, the hope of Glory."

5. Jesus Christ mentioned that pride is the greatest sin in the kingdom of God. After searching your character, do you believe that you have pride in you? If so, what action(s) have you taken to help you eliminate it from your life?

6. List as many responsibilities of an earthly diplomat who represents any nation and relate it to your duties as an ambassador of God's kingdom. Then ask the Lord for grace to fulfill this noble role of representing Jesus on earth.

7. List 3 different types of kingdoms and give examples.

8. List about 5 characteristics of the kingdom of God.

9. Fill in the gaps: "For the -------------- of the Cross is foolishness to those who are perishing, but to us, who are being -----------, it is the -------------- of ----------------"

10. As a believer, explain briefly in your experience how you have practically applied the word of God to have dominion over any given situation.

11. Jesus used several metaphors to explain the **KINGDOM OF GOD**. Read Matthew 13:31 & Mark 4:30 and write a brief statement to show your understanding of the parable comparing the Kingdom of God to a mustard seed.

12. In Hebrews 12:28, the scripture declares that the kingdom of God is a kingdom that cannot be shaken, what should be your reaction to any satanic intimidation and attacks on you?

13. Fill in the gaps: "Whoever therefore breaks one of the least of these commandments, and teaches men so, shall be called --------- in the kingdom of heaven; but whoever ---------- and -------------them, he shall be called ---------------- in the kingdom of heaven."

STEPS TO ACTIVATE THE KINGDOM OF GOD & LIVE VICTORIOUSLY

- Acknowledge Jesus as your Lord and appreciate His work of redemption on the cross.

- Acknowledge that the kingdom of God is within you and be aware of satanic opposition wherever you try to enforce and advance the kingdom.

- Endeavor to enforce the kingdom of God wherever you are (i.e in the government, office, schools, university, business, family, media, sports…) You must fill the earth with the aroma of Christ Jesus - **I Corinthians 4:20; Matthew 13:33.**

- Use the scepter of the Kingdom (righteousness) (Hebrew 1:7), to exert authority over satan (Luke 10:19), and dominion over the earth. **Genesis 1:27.**

- Possess the knowledge of who you are in Christ Jesus.

- Be bold and courageous **Joshua 1:8-9.**

- Diligently seek knowledge of your roles and responsibilities as an ambassador of Jesus and fulfill them by being the salt and a light on earth through godly and impeccable character.

- Whatever you do, do it in love; love the Lord your God with all your heart, love your neighbor as yourself (work colleagues and people in your community) and pray for your enemies.

- Always be prepared to tell people why you believe in Jesus, as the opportunity arises.

- Endeavor to always prioritise the Kingdom of God. – **Matthew 6:33.**

CHAPTER 2

UNDERSTANDING THE DYNAMICS OF SALVATION

AIM:

To increase the believers' knowledge of the dynamics of Salvation.

OBJECTIVES:

At the end of the teaching, believers should be able to:
- Define Salvation.
- Explain the reasons why Jesus came to earth.
- Know why and how Jesus saved souls from going to hell.
- Differentiate between natural birth and spiritual birth.
- Understand the proofs and misconceptions of salvation, and how to correct it.
- Explain everything Jesus sacrificed in exchange for your soul and the full benefits of salvation; your inheritance.
- Have an understanding of salvation terminologies and how to lead an unbeliever to Jesus Christ.

SALVATION

What is Salvation?
Salvation is derived from a Greek word called Soteria: which means the saving of soul, deliverance from spiritual death, forgiveness of sins through the shedding of the blood of Jesus on the Cross and the receipt of the gift of eternal life through the resurrection of Jesus Christ from death.

It is essential for all human beings to understand that they are spiritually lost and in need of salvation. Every man is dead in sin and needs to repent, be cleansed by the blood of Jesus, receive forgiveness and live a life that is pleasing to God. All of this can be achieved by hearing the word of God and allowing it to change them through the power of the Holy Spirit.

When Adam and Eve sinned in the garden of Eden, man was separated from God. The death of Jesus was a sacrifice God made to reconcile us back to Himself and His covenant promises to us. Through the blood of Jesus, we have received the gift of eternal life and can boldly come before the throne of God.

How Do You Receive Salvation?

In 2 Thessalonians 2:13, the scriptures declares that: *"from the beginning God chose you to be saved through the sanctifying work of the Holy Spirit and through belief in the truth of the word of God"*. The scripture further affirms in Ephesians 2:8 that *"it is by grace you have been saved, through faith – and this is not from yourselves, it is the gift of God – not by works, so that no one can boast"*

Being born into a Christian nation or home does not automatically make you a Christian neither does having a biblical name like Paul, John or James, having a minister of God as a parent, attending a church for many years and being a Church worker, reading the bible, praying to God and fasting regularly, observing religious rites, bearing big religious titles and wearing certain regalia of authority. None of these things can make you born again or make you a Christian. In most religions around the world such as Islam, Hinduism and others, it is believed that if your parents belong to a religious sect, their children automatically belong to the same religious sect. This does not apply to Christianity, the truth remains that Christianity is not a religion, it is a relationship with Jesus. Jesus explained that the only biblical standard, which never changes, is to accept Him as Lord; that is the protocol of heaven needed to enter the kingdom of God.

Ponder on the following scriptures for better understanding of being born again; Jesus answered and said to him, *"Most assuredly, I say to you, unless one is born again, he cannot see the kingdom of God"* - *John 3:3*. Also in **Acts 4:12** *"Nor is there salvation in any other name under heaven given among men by which we must be saved."*

Before you can be saved, you must repent, ask Jesus to come into your heart and be your Lord and savior, ask for the baptism of the Holy Spirt and promise to serve Him all the days of your life.

In this teaching, we will be dealing with the process of repentance and its importance. These include; What you repented of? How to know that you have been forgiven, how your sins were cleansed, ? Why Jesus come to this sinful world, Why Jesus saved your soul from perishing?, How Jesus saved you, What are the proofs that you have been saved?, What did He accomplish for you on the cross?.

What does it mean to believe and be justified with the heart or confess and be saved with your mouth? - Romans 10:10 ; What is the baptism of the Holy Spirit? What happened in your spirit and soul during the process of salvation? What is the significance of water baptism after your salvation? We will try to answer these questions in order to bring clarity to the process of salvation.

In the next section, we will explain how Jesus used different parables to explain the meaning of salvation of souls.

SECTION B

Jesus used many parables to explain and bring clarity to the gift of salvation, here are some of the parables.

(1) Parable of the Lost Sheep - Luke 15:1-7

Jesus stressed the importance of one soul to God and the joy in heaven over the restoration of a lost soul into kingdom of God.

(2) Parable of the Lost Coin - Luke 15:8-10

There is more joy in the presence of the angels of God over one sinner who repents and is brought back into the kingdom of God.

(3) Parable of the Lost Son - Luke 15:11-32

The following is a summary of the parable of the lost son in relation to salvation of souls:

- Unbelievers are disconnected from the heavenly Father due to sins of rebellion and disobedience.
- Conviction of sin by the Holy Spirit begins in the heart.
- The lost son (unbeliever) repented of his sins.
- His soul was restored and he continued to enjoy the abundant blessings in the kingdom of God.
- God and the angels in heaven rejoiced over the lost son (unbeliever) who was saved from going to hell.

(4) Parable of the Sower - Matthew 13:3-23

JESUS EXPLAINS EVANGELISM THROUGH THE PARABLE OF THE SOWER

In **Matthew 13:3-23** Jesus explains the process of evangelism through this parable.

The **SOWER** (the believer) **SOWS** (preaches) the **SEED** (the word of God), the Holy Spirit waters it, (John 16:8-16); it germinates and grows in the **SOIL** (the heart of the unbeliever); the believer reaps the **harvest** (the soul of the unbeliever who accepts Jesus as Lord and Saviour). The harvest is brought into the Kingdom of God (Church) to be cleaned (process of deliverance and transformation through the renewal of the mind- Romans 12:1-2), nurtured in the word of God and discipled to grow into spiritual maturity.

(i) THE SEED FELL ON THE WAYSIDE AND THE BIRDS CAME AND DEVOURED THEM

INTERPRETATION – Matthew 13:19.
The hearer heard the word, his mind was attacked with doubts from satan; and he failed to accept Christ.

(ii) THE SEED FELL ON STONY PLACES, NOT MUCH SOIL, SUNSHINE SCORCHED IT, IT HAD NO ROOT AND WITHERED.

INTERPRETATION – Matthew 13: 20-21.
The hearer heard the word, accepted Christ – become born again, but was not baptized in the Holy Spirit; hence he had no power to withstand the onslaught of a satanic attack (Persecution, temptation, tribulation e.t.c). There was no fruit of the Holy Spirit- patience; he immediately backslid.

(iii) THE SEED FELL AMONG THORNS, THE THORNS SPRING UP AND CHOCKED IT

INTERPRETATION – Matthew 13: 22.
The Hearer heard the word, become born again, was baptized in the Holy Spirit, but put the cares of this world (including material things, rat race – your career which is consuming most of your time etc) above spiritual things (i.e. getting more knowledge and understanding of the call of God, discovery of his ministry gifts and spiritual gifts with its applications). In other words, he put everyone and everything above Christ which eventually made him loose sight of what is important until he eventually

backslid. To be an effective Christian, JESUS MUST BE LORD over your life, and take priority over all others.

(iv) THE SEED FELL ON GOOD GROUND AND YIELDED A CROP (100, 60, 30 folds)

INTERPRETATION – Matthew 13: 23.
The hearer heard the word, became born again, was baptized in the Holy Spirit, become obedient to God, utilized his ministry and spiritual gifts effectively, won souls (unbelievers) into the Church, participated in nurturing, training and sending out the new souls to witness and bore 100, 60, 30 fold fruits. He stored crowns of righteousness for himself in heaven which he will receive on judgement day.

SECTION C

These are some of the reasons Jesus came to earth:

(I) Jesus came to destroy the works of satan (pain, sorrow, sicknesses, deception, diseases, poverty and lack) *"…That He might destroy the works of the Devil"* - **I John 3:8.**

(ii) Jesus came to be a sin offering for the world (He sacrificed His life) *"…He was sent to be a sin offering for us"* - **Romans 8:3-4.**

(iii) Jesus came to save the world from going to hell
"God did not send Him to condemn the world, but to save the world through Him" - **John 3:17.**

(iv) Jesus was perfected through suffering in order to bring believers to glory *"God made Jesus perfect through suffering by bringing many sons to glory"* - **Hebrews 2:10.**

(v) Jesus came to serve and give His life as ransom (money paid out to secure the release of the oppressed) for all those held bound by the devil. - **Mark 10:45.**

(vi) Jesus came to redeem us and purify believers "Jesus gave Himself for us, that He might redeem (buy back from satanic control, by paying a ransom) us from every lawless deed (deliverance from sinful nature acquired during the fall of Adam) and purify for Himself (conformity to His image) His own special people, zealous for good works (divine assignment for individuals and corporately)." **- Titus 2:14.**

(vii) Jesus came to break all the curses of the law(poverty, lack, diseases) by taking those curses to the Cross. *"Jesus came to redeem us from the curse of the law, having become a curse for us, cursed is anyone who hangs on the tree that the blessings of Abraham might come upon the Gentiles in Christ Jesus, that we might receive the promise of the Spirit"* **- Galatians 3:13.**

(viii) *"For the Son of man has come to save that which was lost"* **- Matthew 18:11.**

(ix) *"I have come as a light into the world, that whosoever believes in Me should not abide in darkness"* **- John 12:46.**

(x) *"I have come that they may have life and that they may have it more abundantly"* **- John 10:10b.**

(xi) *"For I have come down from heaven not to do my own will, but the will of Him who sent me"* **- John 6:38.**

SECTION D

These are some of the reasons Jesus saved your soul from hell:

(i) Jesus saved your soul to show His love for you - **John 15:13-14.**
(ii) Jesus saved your soul to give you eternal life.
(iii) Jesus saved your soul to give you the opportunity to know the only true God and Jesus His Son - **John 17:3.**
(iv) Jesus saved your soul to show you His Glory - **John 17: 24.**
(v) Jesus saved your soul because He wants you to be with Him in heaven - **John 17:24.**

(vi) Jesus saved your soul to help you to navigate through the landmines of life on earth - **John 14:17:15.**

(vii) Jesus saved your soul to empower you to claim your heavenly and earthly inheritances.

(viii) Jesus saved your soul because God desires you and all people to be saved - **1 Timothy 2:4.**

(ix) Jesus saved your soul because God destined you to be conformed to the image of Jesus - **Romans 8:29**.

(x) Jesus saved your soul to eventually conform to His glorious body- **Philippians 3:21.**

SECTION E

These are some of the ways Jesus saved your soul:

(i) Jesus saved your soul by grace through faith *"by grace you have been saved through faith"* - **Ephesians 2:8**.

(ii) Jesus saved your soul by His kindness, love and mercy *"by His kindness and love, he saved you through His mercy and regeneration"* - **Titus 3:4-7**.

(iii) Jesus saved your soul by removing God's wrath through His blood *"For God did not appoint us to wrath, but to obtain salvation through our Lord Jesus"* - **I Thessalonians 5:9**.

(iv) Jesus saved your soul through sanctification by the Holy Spirit. *"He chose us for salvation through sanctification by the Spirit and belief in the truth; to obtain the glory of our Lord Jesus."* - **2 Thessalonians 2:13-14.**

(v) Jesus saved your soul to fulfill His own purposes by His grace *"He saved and called us with a Holy Calling… not according to our works; but according to His own purpose and Grace … in Christ before the time began."* - **2 Timothy 1:9.**

SECTION F

This section explains the difference between natural birth and spiritual birth, which is very vital for better understanding of the whole process of salvation.

During the process of natural birth, a man and woman come together with the decision to have a baby. The man supplies sperm and the woman supplies the egg. The combination of his sperm and her egg produces an embryo which we will call a **SEED**. Inside this seed is a genetic code called Deoxyribonucleic acid (DNA), it contains the genetic make-up of all the characteristics of both parents (eye colour, hair colour, shape of the nose, skin colour, height, body shape etc) which shape the character and life of their child. DNA also determines the life span, blood type and immunity of the child.

We will explain this process by identifying the contrast between the natural and spiritual birth experience through the seed, the blood, the water, the breath, the heart, the will of God and the parents.

NATURAL BIRTH EXPLAINED

1. THE SEED (The egg & sperm contain the DNA – genetic makeup of both parents which eventually forms the baby).
2. THE BLOOD OF BOTH PARENTS.
3. THE WATER IN THE AMNIOTIC FLUID WHILE THE BABY IS IN ITS MOTHER'S WOMB.
4. THE BREATH OF GOD WHICH IS GIVEN TO EVERY BABY IN ORDER TO START LIFE ON EARTH.

> *"And the Lord God formed man of the dust of the ground, and breathed into his nostril the breath of life; and man became a living being"* - **Genesis 2:7.**

5. THE WILL OF BOTH PARENTS MADE TO BRING A CHILD INTO THIS WORLD (The man and woman decided to sleep together and the woman conceived the child in her womb).
6. THE SINFUL HUMAN HEART WHICH IS IN ENMITY WITH GOD DUE TO SINFUL NATURE.

SPIRITUAL BIRTH EXPLAINED

In spiritual birth, the believer is also born of a SEED, however, this seed is the word of God. The bible explained in John 1:12 that Jesus is the word of God (the word becomes flesh and dwelt among us) and 1 Peter 1:23 says a believer is born of incorruptible seed.

The SEED (word of God) carries the DNA of Jesus. Every believer who is filled with the Holy Spirit has the DNA of Jesus. As the life of a tree is coded in its seed, so is the totality of the nature of Jesus Christ embedded in the word of God (SEED). 2 Peter 1:3-4. This means the divine nature of Jesus (character, power, grace, anointing) is present in any one who is born again and filled with the Holy Spirit. Praise the Lord!

THE SEED OF THE WORD OF GOD

A believer is born again through the implanted seed of the word of God. The word of God declares that: *"having being born again, not of corruptible seed but incorruptible, through the word of God which lives and abide forever."* - **1st Peter 1:23.**

> *"Forasmuch then as we are the offspring of God, we ought not to think that the Godhead is like unto gold, or silver, or stone, graven by art and man's device"* - **Acts 17:29**

THE PRECIOUS BLOOD OF JESUS

A believer is redeemed through the precious blood of Jesus.
The scripture affirms that: *"… and the blood of Jesus Christ His Son cleanses us from all sin."* **- I John 1:7.**

> *"For you know that it was not with perishable things such as silver or gold you were redeemed from the empty way of life handed down by your forefathers, but with precious BLOOD OF CHRIST, a lamb without blemish or wrinkle"* **- 1 Peter 1:18-19.**

THE WILL OF GOD THE FATHER

A believer is born out of the will of God the Father
The bible explains that: *"Out of His own will He brought us forth by the word of truth, that we might be a kind of first fruits of His creatures"* - **James 1:18.**

> *"who were born, not of blood, nor of the will of the flesh, nor of the will of man, but of God"* **- John 1:13.**

THE BREATH OF THE HOLY SPIRIT AT BAPTISM

A believer is born and given the breath of God through His Spirit that releases divine empowerment to receive life.

> *"Jesus answered, "Most assuredly, I say to you, unless one is born of water and the Spirit, he cannot enter the Kingdom of God, that which is born of the flesh is flesh, and that which is born of the Spirit is spirit"* **- John 3:5-6.**

THE WATER OF REGENERATION

A believer is born through the washing with water by the Holy Spirit.

The scripture emphasized that: *"…He saved us, through the washing of regeneration and renewing of the Holy Spirit whom He poured out on us abundantly through Jesus Christ our Saviour"* - **Titus 3:5-6** (For further study - John 3:5-7; Ezekiel 36:25-27)

WHAT HAPPENS TO YOUR SPIRIT AT SALVATION?

Regeneration of the spirit. The term regeneration is explained in this way:

REGENERATION (Greek: PALINGENESIA).

GENNAO - To be born; (REGENESIS - A new beginning) it means a spiritual rebirth, a new birth.

To regenerate is to form something or to bring something into existence again.

Regeneration is therefore a divine act where a sinner who repents is reborn spiritually and brought into union (his spirit connects with the Spirit of God) with God and becomes a member of the household of God.

A NEW HEART FROM GOD

Every believer receives a new and incorruptible heart from God.

The Lord promised that: *"I will give you a new heart and put a new spirit in you; I will take the heart of stone out of your flesh and give you a heart of flesh"* - **Ezekiel 36:26.**

> *"The heart is deceitful above all things, and desperately wicked; who can know it?"* - **Jeremiah 17:9.**

SECTION G

This section is a litmus test of your salvation.

PROOF OF YOUR SALVATION

It is important to always do a self-assessment of your spiritual walk with God; a "Spiritual check-up". If it is important to do regular check-ups on your physical body, how much more your Spirit. The bible says *"examine yourselves as to whether you are still in the faith"* A regular self-examination of where you stand in your faith walk with God is very important for spiritual growth and maturity. Sometimes, we get carried away with the cares of this world and unknowingly begin to forget who we are in Christ. A regular spiritual check-up will help reduce and invariable put an end to our tendencies to stray. The best person to help in examining yourself is the third Person of the Trinity – Holy Spirit; He is your Helper and He would invariably give you the most honest assessment of your spiritual life.

Important things to check during a self-examination is - Are you qualified, that is: approved, passing the test, is your salvation genuine? Or are you disqualified, that is: unapproved, failing the test, is your salvation counterfeit? The word of God provides us with ways to examine ourselves- 2 Corinthians 13:3 says *"Since you seek a proof of Christ speaking in me, who is not weak towards you, but mighty in you."*

Also, 2 Corinthians 13:5-6 says *"Examine yourselves as to whether you are in the faith. Test yourselves. Do you not know yourselves, that Christ is in you? Unless indeed you are disqualified. But I trust that you will know that we are not disqualified.*

Bearing in mind the warning from our Lord Jesus in Matthew 7:21-23; Jesus said *"Not everyone who says to Me, 'Lord, Lord,' shall enter the Kingdom of heaven, but he who does the will of My Father in heaven. Many will say to me in that day, 'Lord, Lord, have we not prophesied in Your name, cast out demons in Your name, and done many wonders in Your name?'. And I will declare to them, 'I never knew you; depart from Me, you who practice lawlessness!"*

Therefore, you need to ask yourself these questions and answer them truthfully because your answers have eternal consequences.

1. Do you have knowledge and understanding of the gospel of Jesus and salvation?
2. Do you have an assurance of salvation? If not, explain.
3. Have you genuinely repented of your sins before the Lord and received salvation? If yes, what is the fruit of your repentance?
4. Have you searched through the foundation of your salvation and found cracks or defects in the building? If so, what step(s) are you taking to repair the defect?
5. Have you examined yourself in terms of your current spiritual status?
6. In John 3:5, Jesus said that *"Most assuredly, I say to you, unless one is born of water and the Spirit, he cannot enter the kingdom of God"* He elevated this standard even further, in Matthew 7:21 he said *"he who does the will of My Father in heaven"* Now the question remains, Are you sure you are doing the will of God the Father?
7. Are you sure the Lord has called you into the ministry and are you currently fulfilling it? If so, can you prove without a doubt to anyone who questions you or your ministry? Have you received the anointing needed for that specific divine assignment?
8. What doctrine have you been exposed to or taught since you became born again? Have you been exposed to dangerous doctrines (doctrine of man, Jezebel, Balaam, Nicolaitan) or have you been exposed to the doctrine of God as taught by the apostles of Jesus?

THESE ARE THE 10 WAYS TO PROVE THAT YOU ARE SAVED

1. YOU MUST LIVE A RIGHTEOUS AND HOLY LIFE

Righteousness and holiness work hand in hand, one cannot work without the other. Are you living in the righteousness of God? Are you living a holy life?

What do you understand by being righteous?

> *"But as He who called you is Holy, you also be Holy in all your conduct, because it is written – be Holy, for I am Holy"* **- 1 Peter 1: 14-16.**
> (For further study: I John 3:7; Matthew 5:44-45)

2. YOU MUST HAVE VICTORY OVER YOUR SINFUL NATURE

Do you have victory over your sinful nature? What are the characteristics of a sinful nature?

> *"Therefore do not let sin reign in your mortal body that you should obey it in its lust. And do not present your members as instruments of unrighteousness to sin, but present yourselves to God as being alive from the dead, and your members as instruments (weapons) of righteousness to God. For sin shall not have dominion over you, for you are not under law but under grace"* - **Romans 6:14.**
> (For further study: I John 2:14; Romans 6:22)

3. YOU MUST LOVE GOD

How do you know that you love the Lord? Do you love what He loves and hate what he hates?

> *"Now hope does not disappoint because the love of God has been poured out in our hearts by the Holy Spirit who was given to us"* - **Romans 5:5.**
> (For further study: I John 5:1-2)

> *"Because he loves Me" says the Lord "I will rescue him, I will protect him for he acknowledges My name"* - **Psalm 91:14-16.**

> *"We love Him because He first loved us"* - **I John 4:19.**

4. YOU MUST HAVE LOVE FOR THE BRETHREN

Do you love God and your brethren? What is the proof that you love your brethren? How do you show love to the brethren?

> *"We know that we have passed from death to life, because we love the brethren, he who does not love his brother abides in death"* - **1 John 3:14.**

5. YOU MUST LOVE GOD'S WORD

Do you love God's word? How? Read Isaiah 66:2.

> *"Oh, how I love your law; it is my meditation all the day"* - **Psalm 119:97.**

> *"Let the word of God dwell in you richly in all wisdom, teaching and admonishing one another in psalms and hymns and spiritual songs, singing with grace in your hearts to the Lord"*
> - **Colossians 3:1-2**
> (For further study: 1 Peter 2:2)

6. YOU MUST MANIFEST THE NATURE & CHARACTER OF JESUS

Are you manifesting the nature and character of Jesus Christ in your life?

> *"As His divine power has given us all things that pertain to life and godliness through the knowledge of him who called us by Glory and virtue, by which have been given to us exceedingly great and precious promises, that through these you may be partakers of the divine nature, having escaped the corruption that is in the world through lust"*
> - **2 Peter 1:3-4**.
>
> (For further study: 1st John 3:10; Ephesians 2:1-6)

7. YOU MUST HAVE A WITNESS OF THE SPIRIT WITHIN YOUR HEART

Do you have a witness of the Holy Spirit in your heart and are you currently being led by Him?

> *"The Spirit Himself bears witness with our spirit that we are children of God, and if children, then heirs – heirs of God and joint heirs with Christ, if indeed we suffer with Him, that we might also be glorified together"* - **Romans 8:16-17**.
>
> (For further study: Galatians 4:6; 5:16-18)

8. YOU MUST BE LED BY THE HOLY SPIRIT

- Do you know who the Holy Spirit is?
- Do you know how to listen for His voice?
- Do you ask Him daily to guide you in all that you do?

> *"Because those who are led by the Spirit of God are sons of God"* - **Romans 8:14.**

9. YOU MUST HAVE VICTORY OVER THE WORLD, ITS PRACTICES, ITS STANDARD & PRINCIPLES

Do you consistently have victory over worldly principles and practices?

> *"And do not be conformed to this world, but be transformed by the renewing of your mind, that you may prove what is that good and acceptable and perfect will of God"* - **Romans 12:2.**

> *"Adulterers and adulteresses! Do you not know that friendship with the world is enmity with God? Whoever therefore wants to be a friend with the world makes himself an enemy of God"* - **James 4:4.**
> (For further study: I John 5:4)

10. YOU MUST HAVE A SENSE OF URGENCY TO TELL PEOPLE ABOUT JESUS

Are you excited about your salvation and cannot resist telling others about the good news?

Mark 16:15 - *"And these signs shall follow those who believe, in My name they shall cast out demons, they shall lay hands on the sick and they shall recover… and the Lord was confirming the word with signs and wonders following"*

Matthew 28:18 - *"Go into all the world and preach the good news…"*

John 4:25 - The woman at the well was so excited she could not wait to tell everyone about Jesus.

THESE ARE THE CHARACTERISTICS OF AN UNCONVERTED SOUL

(SELF DECEIVED CHRISTIANS)

1. They are after the by products and blessings of salvation rather than the complete package of salvation.
2. They are more interested in what they can get from the Lord rather than having intimacy with him and serving Him.
3. They do not seek after righteousness, holiness and submission to the Lordship of Jesus Christ.
4. They are more committed to church denominations than seeking to know more about God's word, Jesus and the Holy Spirit.
5. They hop from church to church in search of miracles and the supernatural.
6. They are hypocrites and superficial Christians who cannot make a stand for the Lord when facing persecution.
7. They are more interested in theological debates than being taught by the Spirit of God.
8. They do not make any effort to grow spiritually but seek after quick spiritual blessings from teachers who spoon feed them.
9. They are always stuck on only one aspect of theology and obsessed with it, instead of seeking out sound and balanced doctrine through the whole counsel of God.
10. In the extreme cases, some are satanic agents planted in the church, as wolves among the sheep, to pollute, to seduce and cause the downfall of spiritual leaders.

SECTION H

In this section we will deal with some of the misconceptions of salvation and how to correct these misconceptions.

Over the years and in some Christian nations around the world people actually believe that being born in a Christian nation where majority of the citizens profess to be Christians would automatically qualify you to be a Christian or being born in a Christian home, or being a child of a minister of gospel or bearing a Christian or biblical names like John, David, Paul is a license to enter the kingdom of God or attending a church for many years and being a Church worker, following a certain Christian denomination, reading the bible, praying to God and fasting regularly, observing religious rites, bearing big religious titles and wearing certain regalia of authority; please note that none of these would neither enable you to be born again nor enter the kingdom of God. In most religions around the world such as Islam, Hinduism and others, there is this belief that once your parents practice these faiths, you automatically qualify to be a member of that religion. This is not so in Christianity, the truth remains that Christianity is not a religion, it is a relationship with Jesus. Jesus explained that the only biblical standard, which never changes, is to accept Him as Lord. It is the protocol of heaven needed to enter the kingdom of God.

THE MISCONCEPTIONS OF SALVATION

1. BEING BORN IN A CHRISTIAN NATION.
2. BEING BORN IN A CHRISTIAN HOME.
3. BEING THE CHILD OF PASTOR/EVANGELIST
4. BEARING A BIBLICAL NAME (JOHN, JAMES, PETER e.t.c)
5. ATTENDING CHURCH SERVICES.
6. FASTING, PRAYING & OBSERVING RELIGIOUS RITES.
7. BEARING RELIGIOUS TITLES & WEARING CERTAIN REGALIA OF AUTHORITY.

CORRECTION OF MISCONCEPTIONS OF SALVATION

THE ONLY BIBLICAL WAY TO BECOME A CONSISTENT CHRISTIAN IS:
- TO ACCEPT JESUS AS LORD AND SAVIOUR; IN OTHER WORDS, BECOME BORN AGAIN.
- BE BAPTISED IN WATER AND IN THE HOLY SPIRIT.
- ATTAIN PROPER TEACHING OF THE WORD OF GOD.
- GET QUALITY TRAINING IN EVANGELISM & DISCIPLESHIP.
- PROPERLY APPLYING THE WORD OF GOD TO ENSURE VICTORIOUS CHRISTIAN LIVING.

SECTION I
WHAT DID JESUS ACCOMPLISH FOR YOU ON THE CROSS?

EXAMPLES OF THE DIVINE EXCHANGE OR SUBSTITUTION JESUS ACCOMPLISHED FOR YOU ON THE CROSS - INHERITANCE.

He gave up everything He had in exchange for the redemption of your soul. The price He paid for your soul was His death and through his blood you have a new life and a regenerated soul. Jesus gave up His throne and glory for your salvation; these are the privileges, rights and blessings that Jesus gave up for you. The following scripture sums up the totality of what Jesus accomplished for you on the Cross. *"Having wiped out the handwriting of requirements that was against us, which was contrary to us. And He has taken it out of the way, having nailed it to the Cross. Having disarmed principalities and powers, he made a public spectacle of them, triumphing over them in it."* **- Colossians 2:14-15.**

We shall deal with specific areas of believers' life where Jesus paid the price for sins, sicknesses, diseases and illnesses, death, poverty, lack, curses and rejection on the by dying on the cross. These are explained through the following scriptures.

(1) FORGIVENESS OF SINS & RIGHTEOUSNESS

He took your sins upon Himself on the cross to make you blameless and acceptable in the sight of God. Now, when God sees you, He sees the righteousness of His Son instead of your filthy sins. *"For He (God) made Him (Jesus) who knew no sin to be sin for us, that we might become the righteousness of God in Him"* - **2 Corinthians 5:21.**

(2) HEALING FOR SICKNESS AND DISEASES

Jesus paid the price for sickness and diseases with every lash and wound he received on His back and then nailed them to the cross. They died with Him on the cross, therefore sickness and diseases have no power over you. This was prophesied in the old Testament (Isaiah 53:4) and was fulfilled when Jesus went to the Cross.

> *"Who Himself (Jesus) bore our sins in His own body on the tree, that we, having died to sins, might live for righteousness – by whose stripes you were healed"* - **1 Peter 2:24.**

(3) ABUNDANT LIFE FOR YOUR DEATH

Jesus died in your place, so that you can have abundant life here on earth and everlasting life in eternity.

> *"For when we were still without strength, in due time Christ died for the ungodly… but God demonstrated His own love toward us, in that while we were still sinners, Christ died for us"* - **Romans 5: 6-8.**

(4) SPIRITUAL, MATERIAL & FINANCIAL PROSPERITY FOR YOUR POVERTY

Jesus nailed poverty and lack on the cross so that you might have access to His wealth and enjoy it in this life and in eternity.

> *"For you know the grace of our Lord Jesus Christ, that though He was rich, yet for your sakes He became poor, that you through His poverty might become rich."* - **2 Corinthians 8:9.**

(5) BLESSINGS FOR YOUR CURSES

Jesus took every curse upon Himself on the Cross, so that you might be free to enjoy the full blessing of Abraham and the promises of the Holy Spirit.

> *"Christ has redeemed us from the curse of the law, having become a curse for us (for it written, cursed is everyone who hangs on a tree) that the blessing of Abraham might come upon the Gentiles in Christ JESUS, that we might receive the promise of the Spirit through faith"* - **Galatians 3:13-14.**

(6) HE SUFFERED REJECTION ON THE CROSS IN EXCHANGE FOR YOUR ACCEPTANCE BY GOD

God rejected Jesus on the cross because of the sins of the world He took upon himself to give you free access into the throne of God. His rejection was an exchange for your acceptance.

> *"And about the ninth hour Jesus cried out with a loud voice, saying, "Eli, Eli, lama sabachthani?" that is, My God, My God, why have You forsaken Me?" ... Then, behold, the veil of the temple was torn in two from top to bottom; and the earth quaked,*

and the rocks were split, and the graves were opened; and many bodies of the saints who had fallen asleep were raised" - **Matthew 27:46, 51-52.**

I encourage you to quietly meditate on the sacrifices Jesus made for your salvation until it takes root in your heart.

SECTION J
BLESSINGS (BENEFITS) OF SALVATION

Brethren, tremendous blessings were made available to you the day you surrendered your life to Jesus. These blessings are not only reserved for you in heaven, they are also available for you to enjoy here on earth. Immediately you give your life to Christ, you become a citizen of God's kingdom and have full access to all the rights, benefits, authority and privileges of this kingdom.

In Ephesians 2:19 the word of God declares *"Now, therefore, you are no longer foreigners or strangers, but fellow citizens with the saints and members of the HOUSEHOLD OF GOD."*

You become a new creation, in other words you take on the DNA (genetic makeup) of Jesus and your spirit is renewed and empowered to communicate with the Holy Spirit. The Holy Spirit makes your spirit come alive and gives you control over compulsive habits from your old sinful nature. i.e. sexual immorality, impurity, drunkenness, idolatry, hatred, discord, witchcraft, discord, jealousy etc (Galatians 5:19-21).

In 2 Corinthians 5:17 *"Therefore, if anyone is in Christ Jesus, he is a new creation, old things have gone, the new have come".*

You also take on the status of royalty in the Kingdom of God, which is far more superior and of greater worth than any earthly royal family.

"But you are a chosen people, a royal priesthood, a Holy nation, a people belonging to God, that you may

declare the praises of Him who called you out of darkness into His marvellous light" **- I Peter 2:9**.

As a king and priest, you assume a dual role on earth; as a king you rule and have dominion over God's creation on earth and as a priest, you minister to God by offering sacrifices of praise and worship. ***"You have made them to be a kingdom and priests to serve our God and they will reign on earth" - Revelation 1:6; 5:10.***

Being born again gives you free access into the presence of God, no priest needs to offer sacrifices on your behalf like the priests did for the children of Israel. You can access the presence of the Almighty God anytime and any day you like to worship, adore and pray to Him. This was made possible because of the death of Jesus on the cross.

> *"Therefore, Brethren, having boldness to enter the Holiest by the blood of Jesus by a new and living way which he consecrated for us, through the veil, that is, His flesh and having a High Priest over the house of God"* **- Hebrews 10: 19-21**.
> (For further study read Matthew 27:45-53; Hebrews 9:11-12 & Hebrews 12;22)

He gives His guardian angels to every Believer for protection. ***"He has given His angels order regarding you to protect you in all your ways, they will lift you up in their hands so that you will not strike your foot against a stone" - Psalm 91:11-12.*** And ministering spirits to bring blessings to you here on earth. ***"Are not all angels ministering spirits sent to serve those who will inherit salvation" - Hebrews 1:14.***

Additionally, God knew that you will face opposition from satan, and his demon, so from the beginning of creation, He made you in His image **to** have dominion and authority on His creation, including satan his evil works. Therefore it is vital to learn about spiritual warfare in order to enforce this authority properly & effectively.

> *"Behold, I give you the authority to trample on serpent (Devil) and scorpions (evil spirits) and over all the power of the enemy (satan), and nothing shall by any means hurt you"* - **Luke 10:19.**

> *"Assuredly, I say to you, whatever you bind on earth will be bound in heaven, and whatever you loose on earth will be loosed in heaven"* - **Matthew 18:18.**
> (For further study read Genesis 1:26-28; Job 22:28; I John 5:5; Ephesians 6:10-20)

In contrast to natural beliefs, when you accept Jesus as your saviour, He becomes your brother and GOD becomes your Heavenly Father. Accepting Jesus as your Lord and saviour is the only way to become a part of the **FATHERHOOD OF GOD** and be called a child of God.

> *"But as many as received Him (Jesus), to them He gave the right to become children of God, to those who believe in His name"* - **John 1:11-12.**
> (For further study read Romans 8:15; Galatians 4:1-7)

God has a plan for every believer and it is revealed when you become a part of His kingdom. This plan is unique to you alone, it is the original and was predestined since the beginning of the world. The Lord is saying this to you: *"For I know the thoughts (plan) I think toward you, says the Lord, thoughts (plan) of peace and not of evil, to give you a future and a hope"* - **Jeremiah 29:11.**

God Almighty, the master craftsman spent quality time to create you. The bible says in Psalm 139:14 "you are fearfully and wonderfully made".

There is no one on earth like you. He created only one you and has deposited unique gifts inside you. Your gifts have the capacity to bring you prosperity and be a blessing to your generation. Your gifts can be revealed through prayers and the power of the Holy Spirit -- Ephesians 2:10; 2 Timothy 1:8-10)

It is vital that you discover these gifts to find out the call of God for your life, develop these gifts through the process of discipleship, training, equipping, mentoring, and finally to deploy your gifts, and use these ministry & spiritual gifts as the Holy Spirit instructs and leads. (For further understanding and study, read the following powerful scriptures which explain the call of God. Romans 12:1-13; Mark 16:15-18; 2 Corinthians 5:20, Ephesians 4:7-12; 1 Corinthians 12:28, Romans 12:6; 1 Peter 4:10; 1 Corinthians 12:4-12)

You will also receive the following blessings in the salvation package.

THE GIFT OF THE WORD OF GOD

"All scripture is given by inspiration of God, and is profitable for doctrine, for reproof, for correction, for instruction in righteousness, that the man of God may be complete thoroughly equipped for every good work." - **2 Timothy 3:16.**

"Now all these things happened to them as examples, and they were written for our admonition (instruction) upon whom the ends of the ages have come." - **1 Corinthians 10:11**.

(For further study read - Hebrews 4:1-2; James 1:20-26; Psalm 33:4; Joshua 23:14; Luke 1:1-4; Psalm 138:2)

PEACE WITH GOD

"Therefore, having been justified by faith, we have peace with God through our Lord Jesus Christ " - **Romans 5:1.**

THE PROMISE OF FORGIVENESS OF SINS

"If we say that we have no sin, we deceive ourselves, and the truth is not in us. If we confess our sins, He is faithful and just to forgive us our sins and to cleanse us from all unrighteousness." **1 John 1:8-9**.
(For further study read Matthew 26:28; Luke 18:31; Psalm 103:1-3).

RIGHTEOUSNESS

Righteousness is the state of being just, upright and virtuous

"For He (God) made Him (Jesus) who knew no sin to be sin for us, that we might become the righteousness of God in Him." - **2nd Corinthians 5:21**
(See terminology of salvation for better explanation).

SANCTIFICATION

Sanctification is being consecrated, set apart unto holiness; being purified or free from sin.

"By that will we have been sanctified through the offering of the body of Jesus Christ once for all" - **Hebrews 10:10.**

REDEMPTION

To redeem is to buy back, recover by expenditure of effort or by stipulated payment.

Redemption is being saved from damnation of sin through Christ's atonement

> "Being justified freely by His grace through the redemption that is in Christ Jesus" - **Romans 3:24.**

PROPITIATION

Propitiation is an appeasement to avert impending doom. The blood of Jesus was our propitiation to avert the wrath of God upon humanity.

> "Whom (Jesus) God sent forth as a propitiation by His (Jesus) blood, through faith, to demonstrate His righteousness, because in His forbearance God has passed over the sins that were previously committed" - **Romans 3:25.**

EARTHLY INHERITANCE IN JESUS

The scripture declares that: *"Blessed be the God and Father of our Lord Jesus Christ, who has blessed us with every spiritual blessing in the heavenly places in Christ"* - **Ephesians 1:3-11.**

Jesus affirms that: *"Assuredly, I say to you, there is no one who has left house or brothers or sisters or father or mother or wife or children or lands, for My sake and the gospels, who would not receive a hundredfold now in this time – houses and brothers and sisters and mothers and children and lands with persecutions – and in the age to come, eternal life".* - **Mark 10: 29-30.**

HEAVENLY INHERITANCE

The scripture explains our heavenly inheritance this way: *"Blessed be the God and father of our Lord Jesus Christ… to an inheritance incorruptible and undefiled and that does not fade away, reserved in heaven for you.* - **1 Peter 1:3-5.**

The Lord confirmed that *"He who overcomes shall inherit all things, and I will be his God and he shall be My son."* **- Revelation 21:7**.

> *"Behold I am coming soon! My reward is with Me, and I will give to everyone according to what he has done"* **- Revelation 22:12**.

Finally, you have your name written in the Lamb's book of life, so that on judgement day, when the Lord would judge the living and the dead, you will receive eternal life and live with God forever in the new Heavenly Jerusalem where there will be no more pain, sickness nor death *"nothing impure will ever enter it, nor will anyone who does what is shameful, or deceitful, but only those whose names are written in the Lambs book of life"*. **- Revelation 21:27**.

STEPS TO LEAD AN UNBELIEVER TO CHRIST

1. The person must acknowledge being a sinner and repent of their sins
2. The person must believe in his heart that Jesus is the Son of God; He was sent to the earth to die for our sins, He was crucified, buried and resurrected on the third day.
3. The person must confess with the mouth that Jesus is Lord
4. The person must ask Jesus to come into their heart and be their Lord and Saviour. (Read Romans 10:8-10).
5. The person must make a decision to follow Jesus
6. The next step is for the person to receive the baptism of the Holy Spirit, fire and water. (These steps are dealt with in chapter 7 – Doctrines of Baptisms).
7. Finally, the new believer needs to be directed to a Church (Discipleship) where the undiluted word of God is constantly preached for the purpose of fellowship with the brethren and spiritual growth.

SECTION K
SALVATION TERMINOLOGIES

Here is a list of salvation terminologies you would come across in the bible. A good understanding of these terminology will help with your spiritual growth and witnessing to unbelievers.

> *"But of Him you are in Christ Jesus, who became for us wisdom from God – and righteousness, and sanctification and redemption"* - **1 Corinthians 1:30.**

RECONCILIATION

Reconciliation is to make friendly after estrangement from a person to another.

To Reconcile **(Greek: Katallaso)** To mend, restore or re-establish a disrupted or broken relationship between two people, nations or between God and man.

> *"Now all things are of God, who has reconciled us to Himself through Jesus Christ, and has given us the ministry of reconciliation, that God was in Christ reconciling the world to Himself, not imputing their trespasses to them, and has committed to us the word of reconciliation"* - **2 Corinthians 5:18-19.**
> (For further study read: I Corinthians 7:11; Romans 5:11; Colossians 1:20-22)

TRANSGRESSION

Transgression is to violate, infringe on law or commandment.
(Greek: Parabaino) It is rebellion, disobedience and deviation from the true or original direction set by God, to go one's own way.

> *"... to take part in this ministry and apostleship from which Judas by transgression fell, that he might go to his own place"* **- Acts 1:25**.

INIQUITY

Iniquity is unrighteousness, wickedness or gross injustice.

(Hebrew: Avon) It is sin, moral illness, perversion within a human being, which can only be removed through the punishment suffered on the cross by our Lord and Saviour Jesus.

> *"But he was wounded for our transgressions, he was bruised for our iniquities; the chastisement for our peace was upon Him and by His stripes you were healed"* **- Isaiah 53:5**.
>
> (For further study read: Psalm 103:3)

RESURRECTION

Resurrection is revival from disuse or inactivity or decay.
(**Greek:** Anastasis) It is rising from the dead and restoration to life.

> *"Who was delivered up (killed) because of our offenses and was raised (resurrected) because of our justification"* **-Romans 4:25**.
>
> (For further study read: Ephesians 2:6; Colossians 3: 1-4, 10; Romans 6:4)

REGENERATION

Regeneration is to generate again, bring into renewal or existence. Improve the moral condition of somebody, breathe new, more vigorous and higher life into a person.

A process whereby the spiritually corrupted heart of man is re-activated by the Holy Spirit; hence restoring communication with God.

Scripture: Titus 3:5
Regeneration is like a dead battery that is recharged by electric current and becomes powerful enough to move a car or light up a bulb. This is what occurs in the heart of a new believer at the point of salvation.

SANCTIFICATION

(Greek:Hagiadzo) The process of being set apart unto Holiness through the sacrificial body of our Lord Jesus; or to be cleansed from spiritual pollution.

> *"By that will we have been sanctified through the offering of the body of Jesus Christ once for all"* - **Hebrews 10:10.**

Hebrews 10:10-14; 13:12; (For further study read: I Corinthians 1:30; John 10:36)

REDEMPTION

(Greek: Apolutrosis) from the verb: To redeem- is to be freed and delivered from sin; to secure the release of someone by the payment of ransom.

> *"Being justified freely by His grace through the redemption that is in Christ Jesus* - **Romans 3:24.**
> (For further study read: Hebrews 9:15; Colossians 1:14; Galatians 3:13)

ATONEMENT

Atonement is to make amends for or expiate; to reconcile enemies. **(Hebrew:** Charphar) To appease or pacify someone in order to avert wrath or judgment. It is synonymous with propitiation.

> *"And the Lord spoke to Moses, saying: "Also the tenth day of this seventh month shall be the day of atonement. It shall be a holy convocation for you; you shall afflict your souls, and offer an offering made by fire to the Lord, and you shall do no work on that same day, for it is the day of atonement for you before the Lord your God "* - **Leviticus 23:26-32.** (For further study read: Hebrews 2:17-18; Leviticus 16:1-34; 17:1-10).

PROPITIATION

Propitiation is to appease.
(Greek: Hilasmos) It is to avert the wrath of God on human beings by the sacrificial offering of the blood of Jesus.

> *"Whom (Jesus) God sent forth a propitiation by His (Jesus) blood, through faith, to demonstrate His righteousness, because in His forbearance God has passed over the sins that were previously committed"*
> **- Romans 3:25.**
> (For further study read: I John 4:10; Romans 2:5-8; Ephesians 5:3-7; John 3:36)

RIGHTEOUSNESS

(Greek: Dikaiosune) It is being just, upright, blameless, declared not guilty and acquitted from sins and the penalty of sins.

> *"For He (God) made Him (Jesus) who knew no sin to be sin for us, that we might become the righteousness of God in Him"* **- 2 Corinthians 5:21.** (For further study read: Philippians 1:11; 2 Timothy 4:8; Ephesians 6:14)

JUSTIFIED

(Dikaioo) It is to be acquitted from the penalty of sins and be declared righteous before God by faith and through the blood of Jesus. **Romans 3:24.** (For further study read: Romans 4:25; 5:1-9)

RENEWING

(Greek: kainos (new); ana (again)- Anakainos) To make new again; to renovate, restore or transform (A change of heart and life for the better) Renewal or regeneration of the spirit of man brought about by the Holy Spirit at salvation.

> *"Not by works of righteousness which we have done, but according to His mercy He saved us, through the washing of regeneration and renewing of the Holy Spirit"* - **Titus 3:5.**
> (For further study read: Romans 12:2)

REMISSION

Remission is forgiveness of sins and a refrain from inflicting punishment for sins.
(Greek: Aphesis) It is a release from bondage, imprisonment, forgiveness of sins with the added quality of cancelling out (payment for) all judgment, punishment and debt.

> *"Then Peter said to them, repent, and let everyone of you be baptized in the name of Jesus Christ for the remission of sins; and you shall receive the gift of the Holy Spirit"* - **Acts 2:38.**

GRACE

(Greek: Charis) It is an undeserved (Rom 9:22); unearned (Ephesians 2:5 - 9); unmerited (Rom 3:23-25) favour of God poured upon sinful men. It is the divine empowerment given to man to accomplish certain tasks, that cannot be done by human ability – Divinely given talents or divine regeneration.

> *"It is by grace you have been saved through faith, and that not of yourselves, it is the gift of God, not of works, lest anyone should boast"* - **Ephesians 2:8-9.**
> (For further study read: John 1:17; Romans 1:5-7; 3:24; Ephesians 1:6-7; 2:4; Titus 3:4-7; Hebrews 10:29)

QUESTIONS

1. Give 3 reasons why Jesus came to the earth?
2. Explain 4 reasons He saved your soul and why He did it.
3. List at least 3 misconceptions of salvation and how to correct it.
4. What do you understand by the divine exchange that Jesus accomplished for you on the cross and give 3 examples?
5. List as many as 7 blessings of salvation and how you can apply these blessings to your Christian life.
6. Explain in 1000 words your understanding of salvation, the contrast between natural and spiritual birth?
7. List about 5 proofs to show that you have been saved and converted.
8. List 2 parables that Jesus used to explain salvation.
9. Read Luke 15:11-32 and answer the following questions:
    (a) What did the lost son do to be restored to his father?
    (b) What is the relationship between what happened to the lost son and the predicament of unbelievers today?
    (c) Due to his disconnection from his father, the son lived a life of poverty and lack, even though his father was very wealthy. How can an unbeliever be restored to the heavenly Father and enjoy the full blessings of the new covenant?
    (d) The scripture says "the son came back to his senses" what made this repentance possible? And how can you relate this to the

present work of the Holy Spirit in the hearts of unbelievers and those who have fallen away?

    (e)   How did the father react when the son came back home? Relate this to the reaction of God the Father, Jesus and angels in heaven over a sinner who repents and is restored to the kingdom of God?

10. Fill in the gaps "For He made Him who knew no --------- to be -------- for us, that we might become the ----------------------- of God in Him (2nd Corinthians 5:21)

11. Fill in the gaps "Who ------------ bore our sins in His own ------------ on the -------------, that we, having died to sins, might live for righteousness – by whose ------------ you were ------------. (1st Peter 2:24)

12. Fill in the gaps "For you know the -------- of our Lord Jesus Christ, that though He was ---------------, yet for your sakes He became --------, that you through His --------- might become ------------- (2nd Corinthians 8:9)

13. Read Matthew 13:3-23. In the parable of the sower, who is the sower? What is the seed? How was the seed sown? In what soil was the seed sown? Who waters the soil to provide moisture necessary for germination and growth? What is the fruit reaped during harvest and who reaps the harvest?

14. In Revelation 1:6 and 5:10, what do you understand by the term *"He has made them to be Priests and Kings?"* What are the roles of the old Testament priests and kings? Relate it to the dual roles of believers in the new testament. Are you currently fulfilling these roles? If not, why not. List your reasons.

15. Read Ephesians 2:19 and explain some of the rights and privileges of being a citizen in God's kingdom and member of His household.

Understanding the Dynamics of Salvation   63

16. In Luke 10:19 & Matthew 18:18 Jesus explained the authority given to believers over satan and all the powers of the enemy. Explain your understanding of spiritual warfare? How do you enforce this authority for maximum result?
17. Explain the term regeneration with illustrations? How was your spirit regenerated?
18. Explain the term propitiation and how Jesus provided it for us?
19. Explain the term grace, give illustrations to show your understanding and how you can apply it to your daily lifestyle?
20. Explain the term resurrection and use illustrations of the resurrection of Jesus Christ and the eventual resurrection of believers
21. Explain the term righteousness and give illustrations with examples to prove your understanding?.

CHAPTER 3

THE DYNAMICS OF GOD'S WORD

AIM:
To teach the dynamics of God's word

OBJECTIVES:
At the end of the teaching, believers should be able to:
- Identify the principles, qualities, symbols, purposes and characteristics of the God's word
- Identify the person who is described as the Word of God – Jesus Christ
- Describe the blessings achieved from memorizing and meditating on the word of God
- Apply the promises of the God's word to everyday life situations

SECTION A

The scripture declares that in the beginning was the Word, and the Word was with God, and the Word (Jesus) was God (**Genesis 1:3**). He (Jesus) was in the beginning with God. All things were made through Him, and without Him nothing was made that was made (**Colossians 1: 15-18**). In Him was life, and the life was the light of men. And the light shines in the darkness, and the darkness did not comprehend it.... And the **Word (Jesus)** became flesh and dwelt among us, and we beheld His glory, the glory as of the only begotten of the Father, full of grace and truth - **John 1:1-14.**

EXPOSITION OF THE WORD OF GOD – JESUS CHRIST (JOHN 1: 1-18)

In the beginning (before the creation of the world) was the WORD (Jesus) and the WORD (Jesus) was with GOD (the Father), and the WORD was GOD. He was in the beginning with GOD. All things (everything – human beings, the sun, moon, stars, animals, plants, rivers, oceans, fish, birds, mountains etc.) were made through Him (Jesus) and without Him (Jesus) nothing was made. In Him (Jesus) was life (totality of human existence; ability to be alive, live, breath, move, eat, reproduce and have dominion) and the life was the light (brightness, radiance, glory, beauty) of men. And the light shines in the darkness (the sinful world caused by satan's rebellion and his evil spirits) and the darkness did not comprehend it.

Vs 14: *"and the WORD (Jesus) became flesh (God – the Son came from heaven, through conception by the Holy Spirit, in the likeness of God (the Father and took the human nature to identify with pain, trials and human sorrow,) and dwelt (habitation and natural living) among us and we behold (to supernaturally see and view) His GLORY, the GLORY as of the only begotten of the Father full of grace and Truth"*

Vs 18 *"No one has seen God at any time. The only begotten Son (Jesus) who is in the bosom of the Father, He has declared Him (made Him known to the world through His appearance as true image of GOD ... if you have seen Me, you have seen the Father)".*

Moses admonished Joshua to meditate daily on the word of God and to observe (obey) everything that is written in it. Today, every believer is encouraged to take the word of God seriously, meditate on it, obey it, and apply it to their circumstances daily. This is the key to prosperity in your spirit, soul and body, and live victoriously here on earth. **Joshua 1:8** declares: *"this book of the law shall not depart from your mouth, but shall meditate on it day and night; that you may observe to do according to all that is written in it. For then you will make your way prosperous, and you will have good success."*

In this chapter, we will be identifying the dynamics, symbols, description, principles, characteristics, qualities, purposes and application of God's word according to all that is written in it. For then you will make your way prosperous, and then you will have good success.

The bible explains with clarity that the word of God has certain qualities; these qualities include;

- It is without errors.
- It has tremendous power to convert the souls of unbelievers and nourish the souls of believers.
- It is authentic.
- It possess the wisdom of God.
- It brings gladness to the heart and strengthens the inner being of believers when meditated upon daily.
- The word of God is pure; it is refined in fire like gold and is purified seven times.
- It is worth more than gold; it is priceless.
- The word of God has the power of revelation.
- The word of God has more nutrient to nourish the body than the sweetness of Honey.
- There are tremendous blessings promised to anyone who honours, respects and takes the word of God seriously. *"... but on this one will I look, on him who is poor and of a contrite spirit, and who trembles at My word."* - **Isaiah 66:2a.**
- The bible says that the word become flesh and dwelt among us, meaning JESUS CHRIST is the WORD OF GOD!

SECTION B
THE SYMBOLS OF THE WORD OF GOD

The following are biblical symbols used to describe the word of God.

1. The word of God is like gold - Psalm 19:10; Proverbs 25:12.
2. The word of God is like a nail - Ecclesiastes 12:11.
3. The word of God is like a lamp - Psalm 119:105.
4. The word of God is like a mirror - James 1:23.
5. The word of God is like a seed - 1 Peter 1:23.
6. The word of God is like a hammer - Jeremiah 23:29.
7. The word of God is like honey - Psalm 119:103; Psalm 19:10; Revelation 10:10.
8. The word of God is Fire - Jeremiah 23:29.
9. The word of God is like an anchor - Hebrews 6:18-19.
10. The word of God is like bread - Matthew 4:4; Deuteronomy 8:3.
11. The word of God is like milk - I Peter 2:2.
12. The word of God is like meat - Hebrews 5:14.

What is the description of the word of God?

> *"The word of God is living and powerful, and sharper than any two edged sword, piercing even to the division of soul and spirit, and of joints and marrow, and is a discerner of the thought and intents of the heart"* **- Hebrews 4:12.**

THE PRINCIPLES OF THE WORD OF GOD

Every believer is expected to start with drinking the milk of the word of God (1st Peter 2:2); but the goal the Lord has set for us is to reach spiritual maturity by eating the meat of the word of God (Hebrews 5:12-14). This can only be achieved by studying, meditating and applying the word to your life daily. If you stay consistent with the word of God, our spiritual senses will be heightened and we will be able to discern good and evil.

The bible declares that;

> *Blessed is the man that walketh not in the counsel of the ungodly, nor standeth in the way of sinners, nor sitteth in the seat of the scornful.*
>
> *But his delight is in the law of the Lord; and in his law doth he meditate day and night.*
>
> *And he shall be like a tree planted by the rivers of water, that bringeth forth his fruit in his season; his leaf also shall not wither; and whatsoever he doeth shall prosper.*
>
> *The ungodly are not so: but are like the chaff which the wind driveth away.*
>
> *Therefore the ungodly shall not stand in the judgment, nor sinners in the congregation of the righteous.*
>
> *For the Lord knoweth the way of the righteous: but the way of the ungodly shall perish* - **Psalm 1:1-6 (KJV).**

What is a Statute?
Statutes are a set of written rules and laws.

QUALITIES OF THE WORD OF GOD
The following scriptures describe the qualities of God's word;
1. Authorship of the word of God - 2 Timothy 3:16.
2. Authority of the word of God - Psalm 138:2.
3. Authenticity and efficacy of the word of God - Matthew 4:1-11.
4. The dynamics of the word of God - Luke 6:46-49.
5. Sanctification by the word of God - John 17;17.
6. The fulfillment of the word of God - Matthew 5:17-19.
7. Dependability and Reliability on the word of God - Joshua 23:14;

Psalm 33:4; Proverbs 30:5; Luke 1:1-4.
8. Inerrant word of God - Proverbs 30:5-6.
9. Purity of the word of God. (The word of the Lord are pure words, like silver tried in the furnace of the earth, purified seven times – Psalm 12:6

CHARACTERISTICS OF THE WORD OF GOD

These are the characteristics which describe the power in the word of God:
- The word of God gives light to the heart and understanding to the ways of God - Psalm 119:130.
- The word of God is a lamp that shows the way in darkness - Psalm 119:105; The Holy Spirit reveals deep and secret things, He knows what is in the darkness, light dwells with Him – Daniel 2:22.
- There is safety in the word of God- It can save you from danger and destruction – James 1:20-26.
- The word of God is a seed, when you sow the word, you will reap a harvest - Mark 4:14-15; Luke 18:11).
- Believers must be thankful for the word of God - Psalm 119:62.
- Believers receive strength from the word of God - Psalm 119:107.
- The word of God is settled forever in heaven - Psalm 119:89.
- The word of God enables you to stay away from sin - Psalm 119:11.
- The word of God gives life - Psalm 119:50.
- The word of God is truth - John 17:17.
- The word of God are spirit and life - John 6:63.
- The word of the Lord is proven - 2 Samuel 22:31.
- The word of the Lord (Statutes) brings rejoicing to the heart - Psalm 19:8.
- The word of God brings revelation – it enlightens the eyes - Psalm 19:8.

SECTION C
THE IMPORTANCE OF MEMORIZING AND MEDITATING ON THE WORD OF GOD

Meditate (Hebrews: Hagah) means to contemplate something as one repeats the words; to ponder; to quietly repeat a word in a soft droning sound while completely removing outside distractions.

The most efficient and profitable ways to make the word of God dwell richly in you is to constantly study, memorize and meditate on it daily.

To effectively memorize the word, take a verse of the scripture at a time, read it repeatedly and study it. Then close your bible and see how much you can remember without looking at it. Write it down and continue to roll it in your mind (meditate) throughout the day. The next day, try another verse of the scripture and go through the same sequence; by the end of the month, you would have committed several verses to memory.

The Bible declares: *"Let the word of Christ dwell in you richly as you teach and admonish one another with all wisdom...."* **- Colossians 3:16.**

*"...But his delight is in the law of the Lord, and on His law he **MEDITATES** day and night..."* - **Psalm 1:1-4**

Prophet Jeremiah declares that: *" Your word was found (to acquire and secure) and I ate them (to chew and consume and digest) and your word was to me the JOY and rejoicing of my heart (the inner man, thinking, reflection at the seat of appetites) – it nourishes our thoughts, emotions and releases joy"* - **Jeremiah 15:16.**

(Further scriptures on Meditation - Psalm 77:12; 77:6; 4:4; 119:15; 19:14; 104:34; 119:97; Joshua 1:8; Philippians 4:8)

BLESSINGS FOR BELIEVERS WHO MEDITATE ON THE WORD DAILY

These are the blessings for whosoever meditates on the word of God daily.

- You will be blessed (satisfied, happy and live long).

- You shall be like a tree planted by the rivers of water (continuous feeding, nourishment and growth, both spiritually and physically).
- You will bring forth your fruit in due season (you will be productive with the promised rewards from the Lord).
- Your leaf shall not wither (you will enjoy divine health; every part of your body will function perfectly).
- Whatever you do shall prosper (prosperity of the spirit – divine revelation & discernment; Soul – sound mind and peace; Body – divine health, strength, financial prosperity and divine favour with God and man) In other words, meditation on the word of God enables a believer to have an wholesome, blessed and productive life that will bring glory to the name of Jesus.
- Meditating on God's blessings and past testimonies will build your faith and dependency on Him to meet your present needs - Psalm 77: 6 &12.
- Practicing meditation on the word will teach you to be still while you wait for the Holy Spirit to speak to you - Psalm 4:4.
- Meditation on the statutes of God continuously enables you to be prosperous and successful - Joshua 1:8.

SECTION D
APPLICATION OF THE WORD OF GOD

GUIDELINES TO READ THE BIBLE EFFECTIVELY

1. Memorize scriptural verses daily
- Take a scriptural passage for example Psalm 119:103
  "Your word is sweet to my taste, sweeter than honey to my mouth."
- Ask yourself these questions:
  - What does this passage say?
  - What does this passage mean? (interpretation of the passage is necessary by depending on the Holy Spirit to teach you).
  - How do I apply it to my life? (This can be achieved by reflecting

on the success of previous application which yielded a testimony).
2. Meditate on the verse daily for 7 days by pondering on it and continuously rolling it over in your thoughts, day and night. (Read Psalm 1:1-4).

Meditating on God's word is like the process of mastication (chewing) of food in the mouth. When you put food in your mouth, it is mixed with saliva (which is an enzyme that speeds up the rate of chemical reaction) for easy digestion and release of nutrients into the body for growth in every organ, bone, joint, blood stream, muscle and cartilage.

This is also what happens when you meditate on God's word; the Holy Spirit acts like an enzyme that helps you understand, assimilate and infuse the word of God into your heart until it begins to release strength and peace into your body, your inner being and your mind. When you meditate on God's word, it will affect your motives, actions and thoughts. Meditation will also build up your faith in God which will eventually lead to spiritual growth and spiritual maturity.

PRAYER POINTS ON MEDITATION

1. Lord grant me the grace to meditate on your precepts, delight myself in your statutes and to always remember your word (Psalm 119:15-16).
2. Lord open my mind to understand the scriptures.
3. Lord let the word of my mouth and the meditation of my heart be acceptable to you (Psalm 19:14).
4. Lord let your law be my meditation all day (Psalm 119:97).

PURPOSE OF THE WORD OF GOD

The scripture below highlights the purpose of God's word to believers. We will expatiate on each of these purposes to have a clearer understanding of God's gift to us.

> *"All scripture is given by inspiration of God, and is profitable for **doctrine**, for **reproof, for correction, for instruction** in righteousness"* – **2 Timothy 3:16**.

> *Apostle Paul instructed Timothy to do these things:* "*Preach the word, be prepared in season and out of season; correct, rebuke and encourage with great patience and careful instruction.*" - **2 Timothy 4:2.**

Therefore, the word of God is given to us as gift in order to accomplish the following purposes:

DOCTRINE (TEACHING)

> *"And they continued steadfastly in the apostles' DOCTRINE and fellowship, in the breaking of bread and in prayers"* - **Acts 2:42**

What is a Doctrine?
It is a set of beliefs held and taught by a church.

What is Teaching?
Teaching is to impart knowledge with the purpose of instructing someone as to how to do something.

Apostle Paul instructed Titus to do this *"You must **teach** what is in accord with sound doctrine"* **Titus 2:1.** (For further study read Titus 2: 2-4)

REPROOF (REBUKE)

What is Reproof?
It is to reprove, reprimand, censure authoritatively; to chide a person.

> *"Holding fast the faithful word as he has been taught, that he may be able, by sound doctrine, both to exhort and convict those who contradict."* **- Titus 1:9.**

Apostle Paul further instructed Titus on the things he is to teach; *"These, then, are the things you should teach, encourage and rebuke with all authority…"* **Titus 2:15.** (For further study : I John 1: 4; Isaiah 8:20; Jeremiah 23:29-31).

CORRECTION

What is Correction?
It is to substitute right for what is wrong; to set right. To admonish a person. To counteract hurtful quality.

> *"Teaching us that, denying ungodliness and worldly lusts, we should live soberly, righteously, and godly, in this present world"* **- Titus 2:12.**

INSTRUCTION (TRAINING)

What is an Instruction?
It is to teach, inform, direct or command a person to do something.

> *"take firm hold of instruction, do not let go…."*
> **- Proverbs 4:13.**

> *"He has shown you O man, what is good and what does the Lord require of you. But to do justly, to love mercy, and to walk humbly with your God."*
> **- Micah 6:8.** (For further study: Psalm 119:9).

COMFORT

What is to Comfort?

It is to soothe in grief, console; to make someone comfortable.

> *"Blessed be the God and Father of our Lord Jesus Christ, the Father of mercies and God of all comfort, who comforts us in all our tribulation, that we may be able to comfort those who are in trouble, with the comfort with which we ourselves are comforted by God."* - **2 Corinthians 1:3-4**.
> (For further study: John 16:33; Isaiah 40:1; Jeremiah 15:16)

APPLICATION OF THE PROMISES OF GOD'S WORD

These are practical steps a believer can take to apply the promises of God's word to their lives and get results (manifestation).

1. Identify the scriptures with the divine promises relating to your specific need (for example, take this scripture and personalize it.

    > *"Here am I (your name) and the children (their names) whom the Lord has given me! We are for signs and wonders in Israel (your city or country) from the Lord of hosts, who dwell in Mount Zion."*
    > **- Isaiah 8:18.**

2. Read through it several times and ask the Holy Spirit to give you a deeper understanding and revelation of the promise in the scripture.
3. Apply your faith in God as you meditate, pray and personalize the scripture until the Lord confirms it in your life. (Do this for as long as it takes to receive the answer).
4. Proclaim or confess the promises of God daily in every area of your life (health, finances, family, career etc.).

Below, you will find scriptural promises to confess for different areas of your life.

Start daily by thanking God even before you see the manifestation of your confession; this is an act of faith.

Here are some of the scriptural promises in the word of God:

HEALING
1st Peter 2:24
Psalm 103:3
Psalm 107:20
Malachi 4:2

FINANCE
2nd Corinthians 8:9
2nd Corinthians 9:8-10
Isaiah 60:5

DIVINE HEALTH
3rd John 2
Jeremiah 33:6
Jeremiah 30:17

FAMILY BLESSINGS
Isaiah 8:18
Deuteronomy 12:28
Proverbs 3:33

PEACE OF GOD
Philippians 4:7
Psalm 29:11
Romans 5:1

LONG LIFE (Longevity)
Proverbs 9:10-11
Proverbs 10:27
Proverbs 22:4

CHILDREN
Isaiah 54:13
Deuteronomy 7:12
Psalm 113:9
Psalm 127:3-5

DELIVERANCE
Proverbs 21:31
Psalm 18:50
Obadiah 17

PRAYERS FOR THE BLESSINGS OF GOD'S WORD

1. Lord open my eyes that I may see the wondrous things from your law -Psalm 119:18
2. Lord grant me grace to allow the word of God to dwell richly in me – Colossians 3:16.
3. Lord let your word be a lamp to my feet, that I may not stumble in life – Psalm 119:105.
4. Lord enable me to hide your word in my heart that I may not sin against you – Psalm 119:11.
5. Lord do not take the word of truth utterly out of my mouth because I have hoped in your ordinances - Psalm 119:43.

6. Lord, let there be manifestation of the promises of your word in my life.
7. Lord, I thank you that you are ready to perform your word in my life according to your promises.
8. Thank you Lord because your promises are Yes and Amen, in Christ Jesus. I stand on the promises of your word which declares that: **INSERT THE PROMISE OF GOD**.. e.g. *"Here am I and the children whom the Lord has given me, we are for signs and wonders in **this nation** (emphasis mine) from the Lord of hosts. Who dwells in Mount Zion"* - **Isaiah 8:18**

QUESTIONS

1. The word of God is -------------- and ----------------, and sharper than ------------ piercing even to the division of -------------- and --------------- and joints and marrow. It is discerner of ------------ and ---------- of the heart (Hebrews 4:12)
2. List 5 symbols of the word of God. Explain these symbols with the appropriate scriptures?
3. How would you describe the word of God?
4. Read Genesis 1:3 and John 1: 1-14 and explain who the word of God is?
5. In Jeremiah 28:29, the word of God is like ------------------- and what is the purpose of this symbol in relation to the word of God?
6. What does it mean to meditate on the word of God?
7. List 4 purposes of the word of God and explain using the scriptures?

8. Read Psalm 1:1-4 and list some of the blessings involved with regularly meditating on the word of God.
9. List 3 qualities of the word of God?
10. Explain the guidelines needed to read the bible effectively for spiritual growth and material blessings.
11. Search through the bible and identify 10 categories of the promises of God (i.e family, protection, finance …) and how you can apply these promises to your life.

Give a testimony of one or more instances when meditated on God's promise until you got results.

CHAPTER 4

UNDERSTANDING THE IMPORTANCE OF THE ELEMENTARY PRINCIPLES OF CHRIST

AIM:

To impart knowledge and Understanding of how important the elementary principles of Christ is to every believer.

OBJECTIVES:

At the end of the teaching, believers should be able to:
1. Explain the apostles' doctrines and various types of doctrines.
2. List the importance and purposes of teaching the elementary principles of Christ and the repercussion of a lack of it.
3. Define backsliding, its causes, how to prevent it and how to restore a backslidden believer.
4. Understand your position as a believer in Christ and how to apply this knowledge to your life.

SECTION A
IMPORTANCE OF THE ELEMENTARY PRINCIPLES OF CHRIST

What is a Principle?
It is a fundamental (essential, original, affecting and serving as a base) truth that serves as a foundation for a system or belief.

Before Jesus left His disciples, He instructed them to stay in Jerusalem until they receive power from heaven - the promised Holy Spirit. In obedience they waited and on the day of Pentecost, that promise was fulfilled; they were all filled with the Holy Spirit and spoke in tongues. Apostle Peter preached a powerful sermon that led to increase of 3,000 additional souls to the Church.

The bible said of these additional souls; "And they CONTINUED in APOSTLES' DOCTRINE and fellowship, in the Breaking of Bread, and in Prayers., then fear came upon every soul, and many WONDERS AND SIGNS were done through the Apostles – **Acts 2 : 42-43**

The apostle's doctrine is about teaching the counsel of God's word including the teaching about the cross and the elementary principles of Christ.

DIVINE WARNING

2 John 9-11 *"Whoever transgresses and does not abide in the doctrine of Christ does not have God. He who abides in the doctrine of Christ has both the Father and the Son. If anyone comes to you & does not bring this doctrine, do not receive him into your house nor greet him, for he who greets him shares in his evil deeds".*

DOCTRINES

What is a doctrine?
A doctrine is a set of principles or religious beliefs taught by a church.

DIFFERENT TYPES OF DOCTRINES

In this section, we will explore different types of doctrines; their relevance, false doctrines and their destructive effects to the church of Jesus, a warning to avoid them and the impending judgement of God on spiritual leaders who allow these doctrines to contaminate the Church.

APOSTLES' DOCTRINE

It is the doctrine of Jesus Christ which he taught his apostles through various trainings and practical experiences.

> *"And they continued steadfastly in the Apostles' doctrine and fellowship, in the breaking of bread and in prayers."* - **Acts 2:42.**

Apostle Paul instructed Titus to do this *"You must teach what is in accord with sound doctrine"* **- Titus 2:1.**

DOCTRINES OF MEN

These are carnal principles derived from human intellect and are falsely taught as doctrines of Jesus.

> *Jesus said, "And in vain they worship Me, teaching as doctrines the commandment of men".* **- Matthew 15:9.**
> (For further study read: Mark 7: 7-13; Ephesians 4:14; Hebrews 13:9; Colossians 2:8; 2:22-23)

DOCTRINES OF BALAAM

Balaam's doctrines are principles derived from demonically inspired counsel.

Apostle Peter mentioned that: *"they have forsaken the right way and gone astray, following the way of Balaam the son of Boer, who loves the wages of unrighteousness."* **- 2 Peter 2:15.**
(Further study read: Jude 11-13; Revelation 2:14)

DOCTRINES OF NICOLAITAN

NICOLAITAN means conquering the laity; and the word laity is the non–biblical term which refers to the congregation; hence the word Nicolaitan means superiority of leaders imposed on a congregation to control and enforce their own ideology which permits idolatry and immorality.

In Revelations chapter 2, Jesus commended the Church in Smyrna that: *"But this you have, that you hate the deeds of the Nicolaitans, which I also hate."(Vs6)*

However, Jesus rebuked the Church in Pergamum that: *"Thus you also have those who hold the doctrine of Nicolaitans which thing I hate".(Vs 15)* **(Revelation 2: 6 & 15)**

DOCTRINES OF JEZEBEL

These are a set of satanically inspired teachings derived from evil spirits. Jesus rebuked the Church in Thyatira that: *"Nevertheless, I have a few things against you, because you allow that woman Jezebel, who calls herself a prophetess, to teach and seduce My servants to commit sexual immorality and eat things sacrificed to idols"* **- Revelation 2: 20-23.**

DOCTRINES OF DEMONS

These are demonically inspired principles derived from deceived human being**s.**

Apostle Paul warned Timothy that: *"Know that the Spirit says that in latter times, some will depart from the faith, giving heed to deceiving spirits and doctrines of demons…*- **I Timothy 4:1-3.**
(For further study read: 2nd Corinthians 11:4; Matthew 24: 4,11,24)

Our focus for this teaching will be the Apostles' Doctrine which involves the Elementary Principles of Christ.

PURPOSE OF THE ELEMENTARY PRINCIPLES OF CHRIST

In this section, I have highlighted the purposes of the Elementary Principles of Christ to empower church leaders who desire spiritual growth for their members or congregation. This will also help church leaders see the importance for this teaching and the need to evaluate the spiritual state of their members.

This is a personal testimony; recently while I was preaching in a church, the Lord instructed me to make an altar call for backslidden Christians.. Surprisingly, about 12 people came to the front and out of these people, 6 were members of the Church and some were workers in the same local church (among these people, some were backsliders and some were not even saved). This should be an eye-opener for church leaders.

The following are the purposes of teaching the elementary principles of Christ:

- To help new believers have a solid foundation in the word of God – Psalm 11: 3; 1st Corinthians 3:10-13.
- To save new believers from spiritual destruction and being tossed around by different waves of doctrines by implanting God's word in their hearts. etc. - James 1:21.
- To be able to grow spiritually (skilled) in the word of God - Hebrews 5:12; 1st Peter 2:2; 1st Corinthians 3:1-3.
- To reach spiritual maturity in the word of God. - Hebrew 5:14
- After training, new believers will be able to explain the word of God to others with simplicity, clarity, understanding, wisdom and supernatural attestation - Titus 1:9.
- To enable believers harness the power of meditation and application of

God's word to discern good and evil. (practicing the word and experiencing the manifestation of the power in God's word) - Hebrews 5:14.
- To build unity among the brethren in Church. - Acts 2:4.
- It would increase respect for the church leaders and favour with the saints - Acts 2:47.
- There will be an increase in the manifestation of signs and wonders in the church - Acts 2:43.
- To produce numerical growth in the Church and prevent believers from "falling away" – backsliding - Acts 2:47.
- To prepare the body of Christ for His second coming; as a Bride that is Holy, blameless, without blemish or wrinkles, spotless - Ephesians 5:26-27.

REPERCUSSIONS OF NEGLECTING THE TEACHINGS OF THE ELEMENTARY PRINCIPLES OF CHRIST

1. Lack of spiritual growth in the lives of believers and in the Church.
2. Spiritual indigestion in baby believers who are fed solid spiritual food instead of spiritual milk - 1 Peter 2:2.
3. Spiritual confusion and frustration which can lead to heresy.
4. New believers received from evangelism will begin to "fall away" (backslide) because of poor foundational teaching and a lack of understanding of the principles needed to keep their faith alive.
5. It could lead to Apostasy; abandoning and renouncing Christianity. It usually happens after a Christian backslides. The bible says of it is impossible to reconcile these people to God: *"For it is impossible for those who were once enlightened, and have tasted the heavenly gift, and have been partakers of the Holy Spirit, and have tasted the good word of God and the power of the age to come, if they fall away, to renew them again to repentance, since they crucify again for themselves the Son of God, and put Him to open shame"* - **Hebrews 6: 4 – 6.**
6. Believers will not reach the divine goal of spiritual maturity.

In the next section, we will discuss the term "backsliding" and its causes, biblical warnings, prevention and restoration of backslidden on Christians.

SECTION B
BACKSLIDDING

What is backsliding?
It simply means going back to your old ways. For a Christian, it means turning away from the truth of the gospel and returning to a worldly lifestyle. Backsliders can repent after they have been convicted of their sins by the Holy Spirit and continue to enjoy the joy of Salvation just like in parable of the prodigal son - Luke 15:11-32.

However there is another state called "Apostasy":

What is Apostasy?
APOSTASY – It is derived from the Greek word APOSTACIA which means "FALL AWAY". It means to willfully and deliberately renounce and reject the gospel of Jesus Christ. Backslidden Christians who do not repent always end up in apostasy, this is why the bible warns against it in 2 Thessalonians 2:3:

> , "Let no one deceive you by any means, for that Day
> will not come unless the falling away comes first, and
> the man of sin is revealed, the son of perdition"

1st John 5:16-17 also describes it as a sin that leads to death. *"If anyone sees his brother sinning a sin which does not lead to death, he will ask and he will give him life for those who commit sin not leading to death. There is a sin leading to death. I do not say he should pray about that."*

Examples of people in the bible who fell into the state of Apostasy due to disobedience, greed, satanic manipulation are Judas Iscariot and King Saul. Judas Iscariot's fall was also a fulfillment of prophesy in addition to other sins listed above.

> *"Even my own familiar friend in whom I trusted, who ate my bread, has lifted up his heel against me."* - **Psalm 41:9**

> *"And Judas Iscariot who betrayed Him"* - **Matthew 10:4.**

> *"Men and brethren, this scripture had to be fulfilled, which the Holy Spirit spoke before…"* - **Acts 1:15-25.**

UNDERSTANDING THE CAUSES OF BACKSLIDING

These are some of the reasons why people backslide in the body of Christ.

1. Lack of meditation on the word of God - Psalm 1:1-4.
2. Insufficient knowledge of God's word - Hosea 4:6.
3. Ignorance of your identity in Christ Jesus - 1Peter 2:9.
4. No solid spiritual foundation after being saved - Psalm 11:1.
5. Minimal knowledge of the elementary principles of Christ.
6. Lack of fellowship with other believers - Hebrews 10:24-25.
7. Spiritual constipation - when a new believer is being fed strong meat from the word instead the milk - Hebrews 5:13-14.
8. Prayerlessness and lack of spiritual watchfulness - Luke 22:39-46.
9. Disobeying divine instructions and ignoring the leading of the Holy Spirit - Acts 5:32; Hebrews 5:9.
10. Lukewarmness - Lack of fervency in serving the Lord - Revelation 3:14-22.

11. Pride, resistance to spiritual leadership and rejection of spiritual guidance - 1 Timothy 3:6; Proverbs 16:18; 18:12.
12. Worldly companionship (Refusal to separate from worldly relationships after being born again) - 2 Corinthians 6:14-18; 1 John 2:15-17; 1 Corinthians 15:33.
13. Living unholy lives lead to powerless Christians, unanswered prayers (1 Peter 1:15-16); and spiritual frustration.
14. Lack of love between spiritual leaders and their congregation.
15. Unwillingness to submit to prayers for deliverance from past sins.

DIVINE WARNINGS & CONSEQUENCES OF BACKSLIDING

The word of God provides counsel against the things that can make a believer backslide and the consequences of backsliding.

These are the group of people on the danger list of "falling away."

1. Those whose love have waxed cold due to persecution from unbelievers, attachment to worldly pleasures, disappointments etc. - Matthew 24:12.
2. Believers who constantly look back to the world. *"But Jesus said to him, "No one, having put his hand to the plow, and looking back, is fit for the kingdom of God."* **- Luke 9:62.** (Also read Luke 17:32)
3. Believers who draw back into perdition - Hebrews 10:39.
4. Believers who bear no fruit in their service to the Lord. (John 15: 2 and 6)

These are the consequences of backsliding;
1. Your faith will be shipwrecked - 1 Timothy 1:18-19.
2. God will have no pleasure in you - Hebrews 10:38.
3. Your latter end will be worse than your beginning - 2 Peter 2:20-22.
4. Your name will be removed from the Lamb's book of Life – Exodus

32:30-33; Revelation 3:5; 20: 6-15; 22:18; Acts 1:18-22; Psalms 69:25-28.

STEPS TO RESTORE A BACKSLIDDEN CHRISTIAN

The first step to restoring a believer who has backslidden is to embrace them with the love of Christ. As a spiritual leader, you are not to judge them but show them the right path with love.

These are the steps a penitent backslidden believer should take to be restored:

- Rededicate your life to Jesus by following the steps to repentance.
- Ask for a fresh baptism of the Holy Spirit and fire. This is needed to serve God effectively.
- Ask for great grace never to backslide again, for endurance to run the race to the end and to make heaven.
- Meditate daily on the word of God; find out God's divine instructions and obey them totally. Search out His promises and apply them to your daily life.
- Spend quality time in the presence of God daily through worship and prayer.
- Do not neglect the gathering of saints (in other words, attend Church services, bible studies and prayer meetings regularly).
- Find out the divine assignment the Lord has for you, get proper training for your assignment and do the work with all your heart and you will experience tremendous joy.
- Create time to witness to unbelievers.

SECTION C
YOUR IDENTITY IN CHRIST JESUS

It is vital for all believers to have a deep knowledge and understanding of who they are in Christ Jesus. This will solve the problem of identity crisis affecting the body of Christ.

The responsibility of teaching believers about their identity falls on all spiritual leaders in every capacity. If the believers understand who they are, many problems in the body of Christ will be solved.

The following scriptures will explain your identity(who you are) in Christ; they will build up your faith and give you the confidence to boldly approach the throne room of God in reverence through your worship and prayers

1. You are created in God's image with His authority over His creation - Genesis 1:26.
2. You are born again with an incorruptible SEED. - 1 Peter 1:23.
3. You have been made a King and Priest unto God . - Revelation 1:5.
4. You are spiritually seated with Christ Jesus in heavenly places - Ephesians 2:6.
5. You are a citizen with God's people and member of God's household - Ephesians 2:10.
6. You are a Royal Priesthood - 1Peter 2:9.
7. You are the temple of God and the Spirit of God lives in you - 1 Corinthians 3:16; 1 Corinthians 6:19-20.
8. You have unlimited access to the throne room of God; as a child or a prince approaching the King's throne - Hebrews 10:19.
9. God has written your name in the palm of His hands and nothing can separate you from the love of God – Romans 8:38-39; Isaiah 49:16.
10. You were fearfully and wonderfully made - Psalm 139: 14-16.
11. God gave you the right to be called His son - John 1:12.
12. You are God's workmanship – His work of art because He is the master designer and creator - Ephesians 2:10.
13. You are the apple of God's eyes - Zechariah 2:8; Psalm 17:8.
14. God's love for you is so deep; neither death nor life can separate you from the love of God which is in Christ Jesus - Romans 8:38-39.
15. You are one of God's people, called by God's name - 2 Chronicles 7:14.
16. You are not created by accident; , you are on earth by God's divine plan and He has a purpose for your life. It was prepared in advance

even before you were born - Jeremiah 29:11.

THE RESULT OF KNOWING YOUR IDENTITY IN CHRIST

1. It will solve the problem of inferiority complex amongst believers(due to insecurity and lack of knowledge of the word of God).; believers will be bold enough to stand for what is right and there will be a clear distinction between an unbeliever and a believer.
2. You will have the boldness to access the throne room of God as you meditate on the cost of the sacrifice Jesus made for you on the cross with His body and blood.
3. Courage and strength will spring up from within you to stand for Christ in the face of false accusations, torment and ridicule from unbelievers and persecution from satan and evil spirits.
4. Your approval and sense of worth will come from only Jesus, hence you will fear no man.
5. You will have peace from the storms of life because you have an assurance that God who called you and gave you this divine assignment would faithfully provide the tools to accomplish it.
6. Your identity gives you confidence in God's love for you. You will never doubt that nothing can separate you from the Love of God in Christ Jesus.
7. Your heart will always be at rest because you know without a doubt that you have a Father who hears your cry and is always ready to answer your prayers.

QUESTIONS

1. Define the term backsliding.
2. In 1000 words, explain that the causes of backsliding and prevention of backsliding.
3. How can a backslidden Christian be restored to God? List some of the steps to restoration.
4. List 5 important reasons why the elementary principles of christ must be taught in Churches across the world as a biblical foundation for new Believers.
5. List 3 major repercussions for not teaching the whole counsel of the word of God in the Church.
6. How can the problems of identity crisis be solved in the body of Christ? List 3 ways to solve this problem.
7. Explain how the knowledge of who you are in Christ can help you in your daily Christian walk.
8. Knowing that you are "God's workmanship", how would you approach finding out the divine assignment God has for you? (Ephesians 2:8-10)
9. List 3 outcomes of knowing who you are in Christ Jesus?
10. What is a Doctrine?
11. Explain 6 different types of doctrines, use bible verses to explain your answer.

12. What are the consequences of teaching ungodly doctrines in the Church?
13. What steps can you take to prevent these false doctrines from affecting the body of Christ negatively?

CHAPTER 5

THE ELEMENTARY PRINCIPLES OF CHRIST

"Therefore, leaving the discussion of the Elementary Principles of Christ, let us go on to perfection (maturity), not laying again the FOUNDATION OF REPENTANCE FROM DEAD WORKS; OF FAITH IN GOD; OF DOCTRINES OF BAPTISMS; OF THE LAYING ON OF HANDS; OF RESURRECTION OF THE DEAD AND OF ETERNAL JUDGEMENT" **- Hebrews 6:1-2.**

FOUNDATION OF REPENTANCE FROM DEAD WORKS

AIM:

To help believers attain a deeper understanding of repentance from dead works.

OBJECTIVES:

At the end of the teaching, believers should:

- Have a deep understanding of the definition and the process of repentance.
- Understand the purpose of repentance, what to repent of, who should repent, the blessings of repentance, deliverance from dead works, fruits of repentance, the prayers for repentance and characteristics of those who have reached the limit of repentance.
- Understand the Purpose of forgiveness, blessings of forgiveness and repercussions of un forgiveness

What is a Foundation?

As stated in Chapter 1, a foundation is a solid ground or base on which a building rests or a body or ground on which other parts are overlaid.

Spiritually, a foundation is the underlying principles governing something, a church or an organization.

For the purpose of this discussion we will define a foundation as the life principles God has made available in His word on which you must base your Christian life.

Jesus used the parable of the wise and foolish builders to explain the importance of a solid foundation in the life of a Christian. (**Luke 6:46-49**)

The wise man is a type of Christian who wants to build a house(spiritual growth). He lays a solid foundation by digging deep into the ground until he hit a rock (consistent study of God's word with help from the Holy Spirit and anointed teachers). He laid the foundation of his building (spiritual growth) on the rock he found (Jesus Christ).

There was a storm (trials, testing, tribulation, persecution, exposure to wrong doctrines and heresies) that beat on the house he had built, but his house was not shaken(his faith remained steadfast) because it was built on a solid foundation(sound biblical principles).

The foolish man is another type of Christian who built his house(spiritual growth) on sand(false doctrines, hearsay, no knowledge of God's word). When the storm came (Trials, testing, tribulation, persecution, exposure to wrong doctrines and heresies), his house was shaken (he lost faith in God) and it collapsed and was washed away with the storm.

This parable is applicable in two ways:
Anyone who hears the word of God and puts them into practice is a wise Christian and builds a solid Christian foundation that can withstand persecution and trials. But anyone who hears the word of God and does not practice them is a foolish Christian who will not be able to withstand the heat of persecutions and trials.

REPENTANCE

What is Repentance?
According to the dictionary, It is to feel regret, remorse or penitence about something.

It is to be regretful about something, to be contrite; to wish that one had not done something.

The biblical definition of repentance is to confess your sins and turn away from them completely; this process involves confessing with your mouth that Jesus is Lord, acknowledging the sacrifice He made on the cross, receiving forgiveness, committing to live a holy life by faith and through the righteousness of God.

The bible declares that *"If My people who are called by My name would humble themselves and pray and seek My face and turn from their wicked ways and I will hear from heaven and forgive their sins and heal their land "* **- 2 Chronicles 7:14.**

From the above scripture, note the order the Lord has established in His word to forgive and heal individuals and nations.

KNOWING WHO YOU ARE IN CHRIST AND YOUR GOD

"... My people who are called by My name..."
- 2 Chronicles 7:14.

"For My people perish for lack of knowledge..."
- Hosea 4: 6

HUMILITY THROUGH FASTING
"... would humble themselves..."

"But as for me, ...I humbled myself with fasting"
- Psalm 35:13

PRAYER OF REQUEST
"... and pray ...."

"Ask, and it will be given to you, seek and you will find, knock and the door will be opened.." **- Matthew 7:7**

SEEKING THE FACE OF THE LORD DILIGENTLY
" ... and seek My face ..."

"seek and you will find, knock and the door will be opened.."
- Matthew 7:7

REPENTANCE WITH COMPLETE TURNING AWAY FROM SINS AND SINFUL ACTS

".... And turn from their wicked ways ..." **- 2 Chronicles 7:14**

" unless you repent, you will likewise perish..."
Luke 13:3

RELEASE GOD'S MERCY AND FORGIVENESS
" ...I will hear from heaven and forgive their sins ...."

"I will have mercy on whomever **I will have mercy...**" Romans 9:15

HEALING IS RELEASED ON OUR LIVES, DISEASES, NATIONS, MARRIAGES, HURTS, PAINS, JOBS, BUSINESSES AND ANYTHING THAT NEEDS HEALING AND RESTORATION.
"... then would I hear from heaven, I will forgive their sins and heal their land" **(2 Chronicles 7:14)**

" ... will heal them of their backsliding ..." **Hosea 14:4**

" .. for I am the Lord that heals you… " **Hosea 14:4**

DYNAMICS OF REPENTANCE
The following scriptures explain the importance of repentance.
- *"All have sinned and fallen short of the glory of God"* **Romans 3:23** · *" If we say that we have no sin we deceive ourselves and there is no truth in us, if we confess our sins he is faithful and just to forgive and cleanse us from all unrighteousness"*- **1 John 1:8-9**.
- There is a need to repent and believe the good news because the kingdom of God is near - **Mark 1:15.**
- Jesus came to call sinners to repentance **- Mark 2:17**.
- Repentance and remission of sins should be preached in the name of Jesus - **Luke 24:47.**
- Believers should preach repentance **from sins** - **Mark 6:12**.
- The responsibility of believers to forgive if the offender repents is highlighted in - **Luke 17:3**.
- In the past God overlooked the ignorance of men and has commanded all people everywhere to repent **- Acts 17:30.**

- John the Baptist preached baptism of repentance to all the people of Israel before the coming of Jesus on earth **- Acts 13:24.**
- The scripture further affirms that *"God is not willing that anyone should perish, but come to repentance"* **- 2 Peter 3:9.**
- Jesus gave a warning of judgement if people refuse to repent of their sins **Revelation 2: 5-16 , 22 ; 3:19.**
- Finally, God's kindness leads people to repentance **- Romans 2:4**.

WHAT DO PEOPLE NEED TO REPENT OF ?

All sinful acts and everything that does not originate from faith; this includes dead works which are the works of the flesh mentioned in **Galatians 5:17-20**

WHAT ARE THE DEAD WORKS?

"Now the works of the flesh are evident, which are, adultery, fornication, uncleanness, lewdness, idolatry, sorcery, hatred, contention, jealousies, , outburst of wrath, selfish ambitions, dissensions, heresies, envy, murders, drunkenness, revelries and the like; of which I told you beforehand, just as I also told you in the time past, that those who practice such things will not inherit the kingdom of God."
- Galatians 5:17-20

"Lest there be contentions, jealousies, outbursts of wrath, selfish ambitions, backbiting, whisperings, conceits, tumults, lest when I come again, my God will humble me among you and I shall mourn for many who have sinned before and have not repented of the uncleanness, fornication and lewdness which they have practiced." **- 2 Corinthians 12: 20 – 21**

Matthew 15:18-19 says that: *"But those things which proceed from the mouth come from the heart, and they defile a man. For out of the heart proceed evil thoughts, murders, adulteries, fornications, theft, false witness and blasphemies"*

From the scriptures above, we can define dead works as religious rituals and activities that elevate the works of men over faith in God such as animal sacrifices and all sinful acts.

Hebrews 9: 14 - It is the blood of Jesus that cleanses our conscience from dead works in order to serve God

HOW IS REPENTANCE PRODUCED

Repentance is always preceded by a conviction of the Holy Spirit as mentioned in **John 16:8-11**. *"He will convict the world of guilt in regards to sin, judgment and righteousness."*

The act of repentance involves the spirit, soul and body (confession with the mouth)....

The Process of Repentance:
- Conviction of the Holy Spirit in your heart – John 16:8-11
- Feelings of remorse – **2 Corinthians 7:10**.
- Willingness of the heart (act of your own will) to turn away from wickedness and persistent sins.
- Asking the Lord for mercy and forgiveness - **1 John 1: 7-9**.
- Receiving God's forgiveness.
- A willingness to forgive those who offended you.
- Consecration of your heart and a commitment before the Lord to hate sins.
- Receive grace to overcome sinful nature.

These are some other ways repentance which leads to forgiveness of sin is produced;

- BY THE WORD OF GOD - **Acts 2:37-38; 2 Timothy 2:25**.
- BY THE GOODNESS OF GOD - Romans 2:4; 2nd Peter 3:9.
- BY THE CHASTISEMENT OF GOD - **Hebrews 12:10; 2 Timothy 2:24-25**.
- BY ACCEPTING THE TRUTH OF THE WORD OF GOD - **Romans 10:17**.
- BY GOD BRINGING ANGUISH TO THE SOUL - **Psalm 38:18**.
- BY BELIEVERS SURRENDERING THEIR WILL TO GOD - **Matthew 16:24**.
- BY THE CONVICTION OF THE HOLY SPIRIT - **John 16:8**.

DELIVERANCE FROM THE DEAD WORKS

The Lord in His mercy provided an escape and complete deliverance from dead works; He has promised to fill every repentant heart with fresh anointing and fire from the Holy Spirit that will cause them to bear good fruits, serve him passionately and have a productive ministry.

Hebrews 9: 14 declares that it is the blood of Jesus that cleanses our conscience from **dead works** (<u>dead works of animal sacrifices; dead religious rituals and all sinful acts</u>) and empowers us to serve God. This means, the blood of Jesus DELIVERS OUR MIND FROM THE SPIRIT OF RELIGION fueled by wrong doctrines and heresies.

We are delivered from dead works by keeping our vessel (body) clean from things that dishonour our body in order to be sanctified and fit for use by the Master. It is our responsibility as believers to keep our bodies pure in order to receive fresh anointing from the Lord and be used for His glory - **2 Timothy 2:20-21**.

Remember Jesus warned, *"nor do they put new wine (fresh or new anointing) into an old wineskin (polluted body) else the wineskin (the body) would burst."* **Matthew 9:17.** The word of God further uses a **metaphor to describe the process of deliverance from dead works in Galatians 5:19-21**.

Apostle Paul admonished Timothy that: *"... in a great house (Church) there are vessels (body of believers) of gold and silver (of great worth), but also of wood and clay (of lesser worth); some for honour and some for dishonour. Therefore, if anyone cleanses himself (undergo a process of deliverance) from the latter (dishonour), he will be a vessel for honour, sanctified (set apart unto holiness) and useful (FULFILMENT OF DESTINY AND UTILIZATION OF MINISTRY/SPIRITUAL GIFTS) for the Master (Jesus Christ), prepared for every good work (unique, specific, divine assignment, purpose of God for your life, the work of the ministry)." - **2 Timothy 2:20 - 21.**

In the presence of God deliverance is available to remove sin from your life, enable you to live in complete holiness and possess your possessions.

> *"On Mount Zion, there shall be deliverance and holiness and the house of Jacob shall possess (to take hold of) their possession"* (the full blessings of the new covenant in Christ Jesus)" - **Obadiah 17**.

PRAYER OF DELIVERANCE FROM DEAD WORKS

You may pray like this:

Dear Heavenly Father, I thank you for my salvation, I thank you that you made me in your own image and likeness and I thank you that my body is the temple of the Holy Spirit who dwells in me.

I come to you in the name of Jesus, seeking deliverance from dead works and if, per chance I have opened doors to satan to attack me, I repent and I ask that you forgive me. I thank you Lord that my sins are forgiven, I am cleansed by the blood of Jesus. I am clothed in the righteousness of Jesus. I am sanctified and justified by the name of Jesus and by the power of the Holy Spirit. Therefore Lord, deliver me from all these works of the flesh, namely: **anger, ………envy ……….uncleanness, …….**

According to your word in **2 Corinthians 10:3-5:** I plead the blood of Jesus over my soul in Jesus name. I bring all my thoughts into captivity to the obedience to Christ Jesus, I cast down vain imaginations in my mind in Jesus name, I pull down and I demolish every stronghold of theft, evil thoughts, murder, fornication, adultery, false witness, blasphemies…..over my mind in Jesus name.

Let my soul be redeemed in peace from the battle against me in Jesus name. Let the peace of God which surpasses all understanding guard my heart and mind through Christ Jesus. Lord I believe that I have been set free from all this filth and I thank you for my deliverance. Now, I ask that you fill me again with fresh fire, zeal and new anointing by the power of the Holy Spirit in my inner being. I ask Holy Spirit that you bear the following fruit of the Spirit in me; love, peace, joy…………and the grace to receive, in Jesus' mighty name. Amen! **- Galatians 5:22-23.**

FRUITS OF REPENTANCE & WORKS OF REPENTANCE

John the baptist instructed believers that they should **"bear fruits worthy of repentance" - Matthew 3:8.**

These are the actions that you need to willingly take in order to stop sinning and embrace acts of righteousness, holiness with the fear of the Lord and to bring pleasure to God Almighty on daily basis throughout your stay here on earth.

- GODLY SORROW FOR SINS COMMITTED - **2 Corinthians 7:11**.
- CONFESSION OF SINS - **Psalm 51:1-4; James 5:16; Matthew 5:23-24**.
- TURNING AWAY FROM SINS TO SERVE GOD - **I Thessalonians 1:9; Acts 26:18**.
- FORSAKING YOUR SINFUL LIFESTYLE - **Psalm 119:58-60; Matthew 3:8-10; Proverbs 28:13**.
- HAVE COMPLETE HATRED FOR SIN (Zero tolerance for committing sin) - **Ezekiel 36:31-33**.

THE PURPOSE OF REPENTANCE

Here are some of the reasons for repentance;
- The kingdom of Heaven is near. Repentance is the initial step needed to enter the Kingdom of God - **Matthew 3:2**.
- To produce the fruit of repentance and continue to enjoy the presence and the blessings of God - **Matthew 3:8**.
- To receive forgiveness and cleansing from all acts of unrighteousness - **Matthew 3:19**.
- To receive salvation - **2 Corinthians 7:10**.
- To be reconciled to God and continue to enjoy fellowship and intimacy with Him. **2nd Corinthians 6:18**.

CHARACTERISTICS OF THOSE WHO HAVE GONE PAST THE STAGE OF REPENTANCE (APOSTASY)

Hebrews 6:4-6 explains the characteristics of those who are at risk of going past the stage of repentance if they backslide;
- Those who have been enlightened in the word of God and revelation.
- Have tasted heavenly gifts.
- Have shared in the Holy Spirit.
- Have tasted the goodness of God.
- Have tasted the power of the coming age (Resurrection power).

These are the categories of those who have gone past the stage of repentance and their final destination is Hell

THE FALLEN ANGELS

"and the angels who did not keep their proper domain, but left their own abode. He has reserved in everlasting chains under darkness for the judgement of the great day" - **Jude 6**.

SATAN AND HIS EVIL ANGELS

"and war broke out in heaven… so the great Dragon was cast out, that serpent of old, called the devil and satan, who deceives the whole world; he was cast out to the earth; and his angels were cast out with him" **- Revelation 12:7-12**.

JUDGEMENT OF GOD ON JEZEBEL DUE TO LACK OF REPENTANCE

"because you allowed that woman Jezebel, who called herself a prophetess … and I gave her time to repent of her sexual immorality, and she did not repent" - **Revelation 2:21**.

THOSE WHO SURVIVED THE PLAGUE DURING THE PERIOD OF TRIBULATION AND REFUSED TO REPENT

(Read the following scriptural passages for a better understanding). Revelation 9:20-21 ; Revelation 16:9-11

WHO SHOULD REPENT?

The word of God provides us with information about categories of people who should repent of their sins. They are;

- Everyone and everywhere on earth should repent of their sins - **Acts 17:30**.
- Both Jews and Greeks should repent - **Acts 20:21**.
- All those who have sinned and fallen short of the glory of God - **Romans 3:23.**
- All those who refuse to forgive others.

THE BLESSINGS OF REPENTANCE

These are the blessings of repentance
- It enables a refreshed and renewed heart - **Acts 3:19**.
- It releases the opportunity to receive healing - **2 Chronicles 7:14**.
- It releases God's mercy on individuals or nations.
- It releases the compassion of God on individuals or nations.
- It enables you to receive forgiveness from God.
- It releases answers to prayers - **2 Chronicles 7:15**.
- It quickens the second coming of Jesus on the earth.

FORGIVENESS OF SINS

WHAT IS FORGIVENESS OF SINS?

It is mercy that the Lord bestows on anyone who **repents** before Him as a result of the blood Jesus shed on the cross to avert the wrath of God and for the remission of our sins. **It is to be relieved of the burdens of your offenses.**

HOW DO YOU MAINTAIN FORGIVENESS?

Unforgiveness can leads to hatred, bitterness, rage, revenge, lack of peace, torment, illness caused by the toxin of hatred is released into the body.

> *Do not repay evil with evil or insult with insult, but with blessing, because to this you were called so that you may inherit a blessing -* **1st Peter 3:9**.

FORGIVING OTHERS

Forgiving others must come from the heart.

> *So, watch yourselves, "if your brother sins, rebuke him, and if he repents, forgive him. If he sins against*

you seven times in a day, and seven times comes to you and says, I repent, forgive him" - **Luke 17:3-4**.

Therefore, if you are offering your gift at the altar and there remember your brother has something against you, leave your gift there in front of the altar. First go and be reconciled with your brother; then come and offer your gift. Settle matters quickly with your adversary who is taking you to court. Do it while you are still with him on the way, or he may hand you over to the judge, and the judge may hand you over to the officer, and you may be thrown into prison. I tell you the truth, you will not get out until you have paid the last penny - **Matthew 5:23-26**.

Parable of the unmerciful Servant - Matthew 18: 21-35
Then Peter came to Jesus and asked, Lord, how many times shall I forgive my brother when he sins against me? Up to seven times? Jesus answered, "I tell you, not seven times, but seventy-seven times ……

The Kingdom of heaven is like a KING (God)
- To settle an account with His servants (Believers).
- Debt (sins) of 10,000 talents.
- Servant is unable to pay and begged for mercy; the king had mercy and forgave his debt (sins).
- The servant refused to forgive his own brother of debt.
- In anger the MASTER (God) turned him over to the jailer (satan) to be tormented.

Jesus concluded and warned believers that " So My heavenly Father also will do to you if each of you, from his heart, does not forgive his brother his trespasses" Matthew 18:35. This is how my heavenly Father will treat anyone who refuses to forgive from the heart.

BLESSINGS OF FORGIVENESS

- Restoration of lost blessings.
- Answers to prayers.
- Healing and deliverance.
- Mercy and favour from God.
- Divine promotion from the Lord.

REPERCUSSION OF UNFORGIVENESS

- Unanswered prayers.
- Torment from satan resulting in ill health and loss of blessings.
- Lack of peace.

PRAYERS FOR REPENTANCE AND FORGIVENESS OF SINS

Dear Heavenly Father, I come to you in the name of Jesus, your word declares that all have sinned and fallen short of the glory of God and if we say that we do not sin we deceive ourselves and there is no truth in us, but if we confess our sins you are faithful and just to forgive us our sins and to cleanse us from all unrighteousness. Therefore, Lord I repent of all sins I have committed against you and I ask for your mercy. Your word further declares that you will have mercy on whomever you want to have mercy and you will have compassion on whomever you want to have compassion. Lord have mercy upon me according to your loving kindnesses and according to your tender mercies, blot out my transgressions and wash me with the blood of Jesus. Now I thank you that my sins are forgiven, I am cleansed with the blood of Jesus, I am made righteous with the righteousness of Jesus and I am justified by the name of Jesus and power of the Holy Spirit. Finally, I come boldly to the throne of grace and receive mercy and find help in times of my needs. Thank you Lord. Hallelujah!

Lord, I forgive all those who have spitefully used me, those who rewarded me evil for good I did to them, those who hurt me for no reason and those hate me out of envy. Having forgiven them, I bless them in the name of Jesus. Lord bless them spiritually, materially, financially, emotionally and physically. Lord open their eyes to their own spiritual state. Grant them the grace of repentance and deliver them from the clutches of the devil, so that they will not end up in hell, but make it to heaven. Finally, help them to find out your purpose for their lives. In Jesus' name. Amen.

These are the bible verses used in the prayer of repentance and forgiveness of sins: (1st Corinthians 6:11, Romans 3:23, 1st John 1:7-9, Psalm 51)

QUESTIONS

After reading the teaching on the foundation of repentance from dead works, answer these questions;

1. What are the fruits of repentance?
2. What are the works of repentance?
3. What are the blessings of repentance? (Acts 2:38)
4. List at least 3 categories of God's creation who have gone past the state of repentance and their final destination.
5. Read Daniel 9; do you feel it is necessary to stand in identification repentance on behalf of unbelievers and on behalf of nations, knowing that these groups of people cannot do it themselves? How do you think God feels about this? And how does God react when someone cares enough to stand in the gap for others?
6. Read Matthew 3:2 & 4:17 and explain the importance of repentance?
7. Read Romans 2:4 and fill in the gaps: "Not realizing that God's ------------ leads you to -----------------.
8. Read 2nd Corinthians 2:3-11 and explain the end result of unforgiveness?
9. What is the promise that God gave in 1st John 1: 7-9 with regards to repentance and forgiveness?
10. After forgiveness of your sins, what else did God bless you with according to Colossians 2:13
11. Fill in the following gaps: "Bearing with one another, and ----------

one another, and whatever grievances you may have against one another, even as Christ ………….. you, so you also must do". Colossians 3:13

12. Fill in the gaps- God ----------- all your iniquities and ---------- all your diseases (Psalm 103:3)

13. Read Matthew 6:14-15 and explain the warnings Jesus gave to anyone who continues to hold to unforgiveness. ?

14. Psalm 86:5 says "For you O Lord, are good and ready to ------------------- and abundant in -----------to all who call upon you.

15. Do you need to forgive others who have done evil against you? Do you find it difficult to forgive? If so why? List some of the repercussions that could affect you if you refuse to forgive those who offended you.

16. Why do you need your sins forgiven? Give biblical reasons.

17. What is the process you need to go through to receive forgiveness of sins from the Lord?

18. What is the role of the blood of Jesus in forgiveness? (atonement, cleansing and propitiation) Explain.

19. The Lord …….. not willing that any should ------------- but that all should come to ----------------. (2nd Peter 3:9)

20. Compare (similarities) and contrast (differences) the process of repentance & forgiveness of sins between the doctrines of repentance in the Catholic Church and Non-denominational Church of Christ . Explain in 1000 words.

CHAPTER 6

FAITH TOWARDS GOD

AIM:
To teach the dynamics of faith.

OBJECTIVES:
At the end of the teaching, believers should be able to:
- Define faith.
- Have knowledge and understanding of different measures of faith; the dynamics of faith; the characteristics of faith; various aspects of faith; blessings of faith and practical applications of faith.

FAITH TOWARDS GOD

What is faith?
The word of God defines faith as, the substance of things hoped for, the evidence of things not seen - Hebrews 11:1.

Faith is being sure of what we hope for (from God) the certainty of receiving what we have not seen and the persuasion that God has the power to do what He has promised – **Romans 4:21**.

Faith is total reliance and complete trust in God.

The word of God declares that we should "Have faith in God... Mark 11:22; we need to understand that there is a difference between faith and hope. Derek Prince mentioned in his book: Foundation For Righteous Living that " Scriptural faith is a condition of the heart, not the mind; it is in the present, not the future; it produces a positive change in our behaviour and experience; it is based solely on God's word and accepts the testimony of the senses only when this agrees with the testimony of God's word; it is expressed by confession with the mouth"

Hope in contrast, is not wishful thinking without any foundation. It is the confident expectation based on God's promises (e.g. future return of Jesus) Hope is an extension of faith.

Faith is the present application of grace. Hope is confidence in God's grace and the future manifestation of His promises.

BLESSINGS OF FAITH

These are the outcomes of applying faith to a believers' relationship with God.

- Faith gives the assurance of answers to prayers - Matthew 21:22; Mark 11:22-24.
- Faith releases hope, joy and peace - Romans 15:13; Hebrew 11:17-22.
- Faith gives believer's the confidence to access the presence of God - Ephesians 3:12.
- The shield of faith provides power, dominion and victory over satan and his evil weapons - Ephesians 6:16.
- Faith gives boldness to preach the word of God with the assurance of being an heir of righteousness - Hebrews 11:7.
- Faith enables believers receive breakthroughs and miracles - Hebrews 11:30.

- Faith enables believers to gain access to God's promises through His word, revelation and prophecy.
- Faith empowers believers who go through afflictions to come out victoriously.
- Faith enables believers to turn weakness to strength.
- Faith enables believers to become powerful in battles and spiritual warfare - Hebrews 11:33-35.
- Faith enables believers to receive healing and deliverance.
- Faith enables you to please God and have testimonies to glorify Jesus - Hebrews 11:6
- Faith enables people to understand that the world was created by the spoken word of God.

DYNAMICS & CHARACTERISTICS OF FAITH

The dynamics and characteristics of faith which can enable you to build and increase the level of your faith in the Lord are as follows;
- Believers received Jesus Christ into their hearts by Faith - Romans 1: 17; Romans 10:10.
- By faith believers have confidence in the Word of God and His creation - Hebrews 11: 38-39.
- Faith comes by hearing, and hearing by the word of God - Romans 10:17.
- Believers must live by faith and not by sight - 2 Corinthians 5:7.
- By faith believers apply the promises of God - Acts 27:25.
- By faith believers continue to grow into spiritual maturity - Colossians 2:6.
- By faith we receive salvation - Ephesians 2:8-9.
- Without faith no one can please God - Hebrews 11:6.
- The just shall live by faith - Romans 1:17.
- Faith without works is dead - James 2:24-26.
- Has God not chosen the poor of this world to be rich in faith? - James 2:5.
- The prayer of faith will save the sick and the Lord will raise him up - James 5:15.

- Testing of your faith produces patience - James 1:3.
- The shield of faith is a weapon against the devil - Ephesians 6:16.
- Believers are people of the household of faith - Galatians 6:10.

BELIEVERS WHO ACTED IN FAITH

Several people in the bible who had faith in God are: Abel, Enoch, Noah Abraham, Jacob, Joseph, Moses, Rahab, Gideon, Samson, Jephthah, David, Samuel.

VARIOUS ASPECTS OF FAITH

The following are the various aspects of faith in God's word:

GIFT OF FAITH

This is one of the gifts given to believers by the Holy Spirit.

> *"... to another faith by the same Spirit."*
> (For further study read Matthew 17:20-21)

DOCTRINAL FAITH

Jude encouraged the brethren to contend for the faith in Christ Jesus.

> *"Beloved while I was very diligent to write to you, concerning our common salvation, I found it very necessary to write to you exhorting you to contend earnestly for the faith which was once for all delivered to the saints"* **- Jude 3**.

(For further study read : Colossians 1:23; 2:7; 1 Timothy 4:1; 6:10)

FRUIT OF FAITH

What is the fruit of faith?

It is the blessing received as a result of perseverance, patience and holding on to the divine promises of God's word. The bible explains that the fruit of Abraham and Sarah acquired after several years of believing was a result of their faith in God.

> *"By faith Abraham obeyed when he was called to go out to the place… by faith he dwelt in the land of promise… by faith Sarah also received strength to conceive seed, and she bore a child when she was past the age, because she judged Him faithful who had promised."* - **Hebrews 11:8-12**.

(For further study, read: Luke 5:4-6; Galatians 5:22)

SAVING FAITH (FOR SALVATION)

What is saving faith?

It is faith in the word of God applied by unbelievers to access the atoning work of redemption made available to all who believe in Jesus and His sacrifice on the cross.

> *"Paul and Silas said to the keeper of prison where they were imprisoned "… Believe on the Lord Jesus Christ, and you will be saved, you and your household"* - **Acts 16:31**.

> *"Jesus declared to a woman, "… your faith has saved you, Go in peace."* - **Luke 7:48**.

"... By grace you have been saved through faith, and that not of yourselves, it is the gift of God." - **Ephesians 2:8.**

PERFECT FAITH (Complete)

James mentioned that Abraham's faith was working in collaboration with his works when he offered Isaac, his son to God willingly; the result was the perfection of his faith. *"You see that his faith and his actions were working together, and his faith was made perfect by what he did"* - **James 2:18-26.**

MEASURES OF FAITH

The following are different measures of faith needed to accomplish certain tasks or receive specific blessings from God.

The scriptures declare that *"God has given to each one a measure of faith"* – **Romans 12:3**.

"But without faith it is impossible to please Him, for he who comes to God must believe that He is, and that He is a rewarder of those who diligently seek Him" - **Hebrews 11:6.**

NO FAITH

Jesus rebuked His disciples for their lack of faith because it caused them to be fearful.

"But he said to them, why are you so fearful? How is it that you have no faith? - **Mark 4:40.**
(For further study - Deuteronomy 32:20)

In other words, Why are you not applying your faith?

LITTLE FAITH

Jesus rebuked Peter for having little faith, when fear caused him to lose focus on Jesus and he started to sink in the sea.

> *"And immediately Jesus stretched out His hand and caught him, and said to him, O you of little faith, why did you doubt? (Matthew 14:31) (for further study -* **Matthew 8:26.**

WEAK FAITH

Apostle Paul encouraged matured believers to be understanding with baby believers who are weak in faith, rather than getting involved in debates over spiritual things that are not fully explained in the bible.

> *"Receive one who is weak in the faith, but not to disputes over doubtful things"* **- Romans 14:1.**

DEAD FAITH

James indicated that practical actions must be added to spiritual faith, in order to get the desired result.

> *"Thus also faith by itself, if it does not have works is dead"* **- James 2:17.**

VAIN FAITH

Apostle Paul stressed the importance of resurrection of the dead and that Jesus, being the first fruit from the dead, serves as an example and guarantee for the resurrection of believers.

"And if Christ is not risen, then our preaching is empty and your faith is also empty " **- I Corinthians 15:14.**

GREAT FAITH

"When Jesus heard these things, he marveled at him, and turned around and said to the crowd that followed Him, "I say to you I have not found such great faith, not even in Israel" **- Luke 7:9.**

FULL OF FAITH

"For he was a good man, full of the Holy Spirit and of faith. And a great many people were added to the Lord" **- Acts 11:24.**

RICH FAITH

"Listen, my beloved brethren; has God not chosen the poor of this world to be rich in faith and heirs of the kingdom which He promised to those who love Him?" **- James 2:5.**

STEADFAST FAITH

"For though I am absent in the flesh, yet I am with you in spirit, rejoicing to see your good and the steadfastness of your faith in Christ" **- Colossians 2:5.**

STRONG FAITH

"He did not waver at the promise of God through unbelief, but was strengthened in faith, giving glory to God" **- Romans 4:19-22.**

PRACTICAL APPLICATION OF FAITH

Key Scripture: Hebrews 11:13-16.
These are practical ways faith can be applied to live a victorious christian life.

- Identify the promises of God in the bible regarding a specific situation (Healing, Family, conception etc).
- Apply spiritual perception (faculty of perceiving in the soul realm) i.e. see or picture the promises with the spiritual eyes.
- Have a divine assurance in the word of God (Psalm 138:2); 2 Corinthians1:20 that is: the scripture relating specifically to the promise you are taking hold of.
- Receive it by being assured that the Lord will surely honour His word and bring it to manifestation through the power of the Holy Spirit and the ministering angels of God. - Psalm 103:20-21.
- Embrace it like you are physically holding it. Remember that God calls those things that are not as though they were - Romans4:17.
- Confess it with your mouth by thanking God for receiving it and you shall have it because God has promised and it is impossible for God to lie. This is an act of faith. (I AM CONVINCED AND BELIEVE THAT THE WORD OF GOD IS LIVING AND POWERFUL.THE PROMISES OF GOD ARE YES AND AMEN ....THE LORD HONORS HIS WORD ABOVE HIS NAME... FAITH COMES BY HEARING, HEARING BY THE WORD OF GOD .. THEREFORE, I BELIEVE ....
- Then take a practical step to lay hold of it.
- Remember that faith by itself, if it does not have works is dead - James 2:17.
- For example, if you believe that God promised you a particular job, go ahead and fill out an application form for the job. Likewise, if you are believing God for healing from a certain illness, take a step of faith –practical step by doing what you could not do with that part of your body.

THE RESULT OF FAITH WITH WORKS

These are the results of faith accompanied with actions;
- Visiting orphans and widows in trouble - James 1:27.
- Faith without works is dead - James 2:17.
- Abraham added works to his faith - Genesis 22: 12-18.
- To continue to remember the poor - Galatians 2:10.
- Gifts added to faith given to other believers resulted in a fragrant offering; an acceptable sacrifice, pleasing to God - Philippians 4:16-18.
- Reward of works prompted by faith - Matthew 16:27.
- These are the good works that must follow our salvation - Matthew 25:31-46.

CONSEQUENCES OF UNBELIEF (Lack of faith)

- Lack of miracles - Matthew 13:58.
- Lack of blessings.
- Your prayers become very weak because they are not prayed with faith.
- Lack of victory.
- It opens doors to satan to attack you.
- Anything that is not born of faith is a sin towards God.

QUESTIONS

1. Define the term faith.
2. List at least 3 characteristics of faith.
3. Fill in these gaps : without ------------- no one can ----------- God (Hebrews 11:6)
4. Fill in these gaps: The --------- shall live by ------------------ (Romans 1:17)
5. Identify and list 5 blessings of applying faith.
6. Describe some of the practical ways to apply faith and receive the promises of God.
7. Name about 7 people in the bible who applied their faith in God to their circumstances. Did they all receive God's promises? Identify those people who did and those who did not.
8. What are the various aspects of faith? Support your answers with the appropriate biblical verses. What level of faith are you currently operating in your Christian walk with the Lord?
9. How do you receive faith? Read Romans 10:17 List the steps to increase your faith in God.
10. List about 7 different measures of faith.
11. What are the consequences of lack of faith (unbelief)?
12. "When Jesus heard these things, he marveled at him, and turned around and said to the crowd that followed Him, "I say to you I have not found such great faith, not even in Israel" (Luke 7:9) what did Jesus hear and how did He react?

13. "Thus also -------- by itself, if it does not have --------- is dead" (James 2:17)
14. "But he said to them, why are you so ------? How is it that you have no ------ (Mark 4:40)
15. Read Romans 10:17 and fill in the gaps: So then .... comes by ...., and hearing by the .... of God.

CHAPTER 7

DOCTRINES OF BAPTISM

AIM:
To teach the doctrines of different types of baptism.

OBJECTIVES:
At the end of the teaching, believers should be able to:
- Identify and have an understanding of the various types of baptism.
- Understand the significance of water baptism and baptism of the Holy Spirit and Fire
- Know the Holy Spirit; who He is and why He was sent to believers
- Apply the practical steps and blessings of walking with Him.

What is Baptism?
Baptism - Greek: Baptisma (from verb Baptizo – To baptize) meaning to immerse or dip something.

SECTION A
WATER BAPTISM

Apostle Paul stressed the importance, significance and blessings involved in water baptism; he said;

> *"Or do you not know that as many of us as were baptized into Christ Jesus were baptized into His death? Therefore we were buried with Him through baptism into death, that just as Christ was raised from the dead by the glory of the Father, even so we also should walk in newness of life. For if we have been united together in the likeness of His death, certainly we also shall be in the likeness of His resurrection"* - **Romans 6:3-5.**

DYNAMICS OF WATER BAPTISM

John the baptist indicated his baptism was only in water (**John 1: 26**) but he emphasized that Jesus would come with a higher authority and power to baptize believers in the Holy Spirit. He added that for Salvation to be complete, a believer must be baptised in water and in the Holy Spirit..

> *"I indeed baptize you with water unto repentance, but He who is coming after me is mightier than I, whose sandals I am not worthy to carry. He will baptize you with the Holy Spirit and fire."* - **Matthew 3:11.**

Jesus gave divine instruction to His disciples to go and make disciples everywhere in the world and to baptize them in the name of the Father, Son and Holy Spirit.

"Therefore go and make disciples of all nations; baptizing them in the name of the Father, and of the Son and of the Holy Spirit" **- Matthew 28:19.**

SIGNIFICANCE OF WATER BAPTISM

The following is the biblical standard to qualify for water baptism;
- The individual must be born again to qualify for water baptism (not babies below the age of accountability); however sprinkling water on a baby's head as a form of baptism is not part of the apostles' doctrine, it is a doctrine of men.
- The individual must renounce satan (the devil) and all his ways.
- The person must be taught the significance of water baptism.
- The person must embrace and accept Jesus as Lord and savior
- During water baptism, as the believer is dipped in water and comes up, they identify with the death, burial and resurrection of Jesus Christ. It is a public declaration of the believers' initiation into the household of God.

LIKELY QUESTIONS TO BE ASKED DURING WATER BAPTISM

The Minister would ask:
- "Have you accepted Lord Jesus as your Lord and savior?".
- "Do you love Jesus?".
- Will you follow Him all the days of your life (even through affliction, pain, trouble and persecutions)?
- Do you renounce satan and all sinful ways?

Depending on the answers given by the person to be baptized. If the answer is yes, then the officiating minister would say: _____ (insert name of person) on the confession of your faith in Christ Jesus, I baptize you in the name of the Father, of the Son and of the Holy Spirit. Crowd of witnesses, angels and host of heaven, bear witness to this; thus fulfilling the instruction given by Jesus in Matthew 28:19.

After baptism, the individual becomes dead to self, buried spiritually with Christ, raised to life as Jesus was resurrected and is seated at the right hand of God the Father with angels in submission to Him. The individual will also experience one or more of the following: newness of life, speaking in tongues, burden of curses lifted from them, healing and deliverance from addiction/bondage. At least one or all of these experiences should be expected after baptism.

Some believers will later experience a deeper walk with the Lord. However, it is imperative that these new believers receive prayers to withstand satanic onslaughts, temptations and spiritual pressures. Remember how satan tempted Jesus immediately after He was baptized in River Jordan? The bible says,

> *"He was led by the Spirit into the wilderness to be tempted..."* **- Matthew 4:1-10**.

The devil never changes his tactics, he continues to apply the same attacks and pressure on believers today.

BAPTISM IN THE HOLY SPIRIT AND FIRE

Receiving prayers for the baptism of the Holy Spirit and fire after salvation is very important.

Even the Apostles who had been with Jesus were instructed to wait in Jerusalem until they receive power from on high, the promise of the Holy Spirit, because without it they would not have the power to function effectively in the tasks Jesus gave to them.

The bible described the event preceding the disciples' experience of the baptism of the Holy Spirit, during the baptism and what occurred afterwards; the blessings of speaking in tongues, prophesying and the addition of 3,000 Church members in the following verses.

The bible tells us that Jesus commanded the disciples to wait in Jerusalem until they received the baptism of the Holy Spirit, in order to fulfill Divine assignment He gave to them.

> *"And being assembled together with them, He commanded them not to depart from Jerusalem, but to wait for the Promise of the Father, which, He said, "you have heard from Me; for John truly baptized with water, but you shall be baptized with the Holy Spirit not many days from now... but you shall receive power when the Holy Spirit has come upon you; and you shall be witnesses to Me in Jerusalem, and in all Judea and Samaria, and to the end of the earth." -* **Acts 1:4-8.**

> *"When the day of Pentecost had fully come, they were all with one accord in one place. And suddenly there came a sound from heaven, as of a rushing mighty wind, and it filled the whole house where they were sitting. Then there appeared to them divided tongues, as of fire, and one sat upon each of them. And they were all filled with the Holy Spirit and began to speak with other tongues, as the Spirit gave them utterance" -* **Acts 2:1-4.**

> *"Then Paul said, "John indeed baptized with a baptism of repentance, saying to the people that they should believe on Him who would come after him, that is, on Christ Jesus. When they heard this, they were baptized in the name of the Lord Jesus. And*

when Paul had laid hands on them, the Holy Spirit came upon them, and they spoke with tongues and prophesied." - **Acts 19: 4-6.**

Jesus baptizes in the Holy Spirit - John 1:33
Jesus baptizes in the Holy Spirit and fire - Matthew 3:11

STEPS TO RECEIVE THE BAPTISM OF THE HOLY SPIRIT

To receive the baptism of the Holy Spirit, you must;
- Be born again - John 3:3-5.
- Ask the Lord for the baptism of the Holy Spirit - Luke 11:9-13.
- Be willing to receive Him by surrendering their will and be obedient to the Lord - Acts 5:32.
- Act in faith to receive the baptism of the Holy Spirit - Galatians 3:2.
- Add works to his faith by opening his/her mouth to **speak in tongues** as an evidence of the baptism of the Holy Spirit and as the Spirit of God gives utterance - Acts 2:4.
- Ask the Lord for the baptism of fire and the ability to prophesy, as promised in Acts 19: 4-6. This experience can be attained by laying on of hands or simply by asking in prayer.

BAPTISM OF SUFFERING-DIVINELY APPOINTED OF JESUS AND PAUL

This type of baptism is a divinely appointed suffering unique to specific people like Jesus and apostle Paul.

In Matthew 20:20 - 23, the mother of Zebedee's sons (James and John) came to Jesus with a specific request, but Jesus said to her. **"You do not know what you** ask. Are you able to drink the cup that I am about to drink, and be baptized with the baptism that I am baptized with?"

Jesus further said "But I have a baptism to be baptized with, and how distressed I am till it is accomplished!" - Luke 12:50

It was believed that Jesus granted her request because the bible records that James was the first apostle to be martyred and John later suffered persecution and was exiled to the Patmos Island.

> *"Now about the time Herod the king stretched out his hands to harass some from the Church. Then he killed James the brother of John with the sword"* **- Acts 12: 1-2.**

> *"I, John both your brother and companion in the tribulation and kingdom and patience of Jesus Christ, was on the island that is called Patmos for the word of God and for the testimony of Jesus Christ"* - **Revelation 1:9.**

Furthermore, in Acts 9: 15-16, the Lord spoke to Ananias about Paul's ministry regarding his suffering to accomplish his divine assignment, *"But the Lord said to him, "Go, for he is a chosen vessel of Mine to bear MY name before Gentiles, kings, and the children of Israel. For I will show him how many things he must suffer for My name's sake."*

Apostle Paul made this profound statement in Philippians 3:10 *"that I may know Him and the power of His resurrection and the fellowship of His suffering, being conformed to His death…"*

IMPORTANCE OF BAPTISM OF HOLY SPIRIT AND FIRE

- It releases the ability to prophesy - Acts 19:6.
- It gives the ability to speak with other tongues (Acts 2:1-4; Mark 16:17) Speaking in tongues breaks through the heavenlies to destroy satanic strongholds. It is a language satan cannot comprehend.

- It imparts the divine ability to preach the word of God with boldness and power; which results in numerical growth for the Church - Acts 2:41.
- You will receive the gifts of the Holy Spirit and a hunger for the word of God; it enables the word to dwell in you - 1 Corinthians 12:4.
- It gives the ability to discern and expose satan's secret works of darkness so that you can live a victorious Christian life - Romans 8:9-11.
- It enables the Holy Spirit to help you pray according to His will - Romans 8:26-27.
- It releases fire to burn all impurities within you i.e. anything that does not glorify God; so that the Holy Spirit can make your body his habitation - I Corinthians 3:16.
- It gives the divine ability to cast out demons, lay hands on the sick for healing, and overcome the power of satan - Mark 16: 15-18.
- Out of your heart will flow rivers of living water. You will become a channel of spiritual refreshment for God to use in refreshing others - Isaiah 5:1-5; Jeremiah 48:11-12; Zechariah 2:5.

SECTION B
HOLY SPIRIT

In this section, we will deal with the knowledge and understanding of the Holy Spirit

- Who is the Holy Spirit?
- How does He manifest himself?
- What does He do?
- Was Jesus' promise of the coming of the Holy Spirit fulfilled?

We will try to answer these questions as much as possible. While Jesus was with the disciples on earth, He warned them about His impending death on the Cross with a promise that He would not leave them on their own, he would send another helper; in other words, someone similar to

Jesus, but One who operates differently because He is a Spirit.

Jesus said: "And I will pray the Father, and He will give you another Helper, that He may abide with you forever – the Spirit of Truth whom the world cannot receive, because it neither sees Him, for He dwells with you and will be in you. I will not leave you as orphans; I will come to you (John 14:16-18).

He further said: "However, when He, the Spirit of Truth, has come, he will guide you into all truth; for he will not speak on His own authority, but whatever He hears He will speak: and He will tell you things to come. He will glorify Me, for He will take of what is Mine and declare it to you." – John 16: 13-14.

Note that the Holy Spirit is not an "it", nor some kind of a force, as believed by some denominations, He is a person!

He has a personality and character. He has emotions. He can speak, He guides, He can be grieved, He can help, teach, give instructions and directions to believers.

THESE ARE SOME NAMES OF THE HOLY SPIRIT

- He is the Spirit of the Almighty God - Genesis 1:2.
- He is the Spirit of our Lord and Saviour Jesus Christ - Romans 8:9; Ephesians 1:17.
- He is the Spirit of supplication and grace - Zechariah 12:10.
- He is the Spirit of Life - Romans 8:2; Revelation 11:11.
- He is the Spirit of Holiness - Romans 1:4; Ephesians 1:4; I Peter 1:16; Isaiah 35:8-10.
- He is the Spirit of Truth - John 14:17; 16:13.
- He is the Comforter and our Helper - John 16:7.
- He is the Spirit of wisdom, understanding, counsel and might - Isaiah 11:2.
- He is the Spirit of knowledge and of the fear of the Lord.

- He is the Omnipotent, Omnipresent and the Omniscient God. — Luke 1:35; Psalm 139:7-10; 1 Corinthian 2:10-11.

THE HOLY SPIRIT MANIFESTS IN THE FOLLOWING WAYS

These are the symbols associated with the Holy Spirit through which He operates and makes Himself known to the world.

- As a Dove – Matthew 3:16
- As Water – John 7:37-38
- As Wind – John 3:8
- As Fire – Psalm 97:1-3 ; Hebrew 12:29
- In Tongues of Fire -- Acts 1:8; 1st Corinthians 14:1-33

THESE ARE THE WORKS OF THE HOLY SPIRIT

The Holy Spirit is the One who empowers believers to witness about Jesus to unbelievers, He draws believers into Christ, He pours the love of Jesus into the hearts of believers, He convicts us of sins, he assures us of our salvation, He teaches us the bible, He enables us to live victorious Christian lives and helps us to pray according to the will of God.

- He gives conviction for Salvation (Sin, Righteousness and Judgement) – John 16:8-11.
- He gives the assurance of Salvation to believers – Romans 8:16.
- He dwells in the believers' spirit as a confirmation of being born again – Romans 8:9; 1 Corinthians 3;16; 6;17; I John 2:27.
- He is the author of the scripture (Bible). He inspired the written word of God – Romans 8:9-11; 2 Timothy 3:16; 2 Peter 1:20.
- He regenerates the inner being of believers – Titus 3:5.
- He enables believers to speak IN TONGUES – Acts 2;4; 10:44-46; Mark 16:17; 1 Corinthians 14, 2, 4 , 18. ·

- He dwells in believers –John 14:17,26; Romans 8:9-11.
- He glorifies Jesus -John 16:14.
- He teaches believers and reveals information and the promises of God to them - 1st Corinthians 2: 12-13; John 16:13; 1 John 2:27.
- He bestows on believers the power to proclaim the Gospel –Acts 1:8.
- He speaks to believers – I Timothy 4:1; Revelation 2:7,11,17,29.
- He pours the Love of Christ into the hearts of believers –Romans 5:5.
- He makes intercession for believers (works with us to make our prayers powerful and effective according to the will of God) –Romans 8:26.
- He imparts spiritual gifts to believers for the work of the ministry – 1 Corinthians 12:4-11.
- He calls believers to a special service – Acts 13:2-4.

PRACTICAL STEPS OF WORKING WITH THE HOLY SPIRIT

These are practical ways to work and walk with the Holy Spirit to get profound results and blessings as a believer.

1. BE LED BY THE SPIRIT

How to be led by the Spirit?
- Have dialogue with Him.
- Consistently obey Him.
- Open your heart to be taught by Him.
- Listen to Him.
- Invite Him into every area of your life.
- Ask Him for help and assistance every day and in every situation.
- Be thankful and loving Him by worshipping and singing love songs to Him.

If you desire to be led by the Holy Spirit, you need to submit totally to His leading, be attentive to His still small voice, always trust Him and ask

Him for guidance and direction regarding any issue in your life.

Do not follow your own understanding or usual ways of doing things according to worldly standards, inform Him before you take any action and He will always lead you to make the right decisions **(Proverbs 3:5-6)**.. He will gradually help you overcome the works of the flesh until you start to bear the fruit of the Spirit in your life (read Galatians 5:19-23).

> *"But if you are led by the Spirit, you are not under the law"* **- Galatians 5:18.**

> *"For as many as are led by the Spirit of God, these are sons of God"* **- Romans 8:14.**

2. WALK IN THE SPIRIT

How do you walk in the Spirit? By always asking Him for direction.

Proverbs 3:5-6 says "Trust in the Lord with all your heart and do not lean on your understanding, in all your ways acknowledge Him …."

As you walk in the Spirit, the Holy Spirit will empower you to obey the divine instructions in God's word, overcome sinful acts and be free from addictions that pollute the soul and body.

He will also deliver you from the works of the flesh, warn you against impending danger and gradually help you shift from analyzing the things of spirit with your mind to focusing on Him to guide you through God's will for your life.

Finally, He will empower you to be conformed to the image of Jesus Christ for character development.

> *"I say then: walk in the Spirit, and you will not fulfill the lust of the flesh"* **- Galatians 5:16-17.**

3. LIVE BY THE SPIRIT (Romans 8:13-16)

How do you live by the Spirit? By constantly depending on Him.

As you spend quality time in His presence, He will enable you to put to death the carnal and sinful life and give you the ability to be spiritually alive and active.

Ask the Lord for a teachable heart and He will always be ready to teach you.

> *"If we live in the Spirit, let us also walk in the Spirit"*
> **- Galatians 5:25.**

4. SOWING INTO THE SPIRIT

When you sow quality spiritual material and financial seeds into the lives of believers, spiritual leaders, orphans, widows, the homeless, poor, and into evangelism to propagate the gospel of Jesus Christ, you will receive a great harvest of blessings.

Also, when you sow the seed of quality time into studying the word of God and serving Him, you would reap great rewards. However, if you sow the seed of discord, accusation among brethren, hatred and gossip to destroy the Church of Jesus, you will surely reap a harvest of destruction which can lead to backsliding or even apostasy and eventually hell. The choice is yours!

> *"Let him who is taught the word share in all good things with him who teaches, do not be deceived, God is not mocked; for whatever a man sows, that he will also reap, for he who sows to his flesh will of the flesh reap corruption, but he who sows to the Spirit will of the Spirit reap everlasting life"* **- Galatians 6:6-8.**

5. FELLOWSHIP WITH THE SPIRIT

This is synonymous with the way you interact with other Believers in conversations with each other and in showing mutual respect. Also, fellowship with the Holy Spirit should be dialogue; as you speak to the Holy Spirit, He will also speak to you and give you answers to your questions. The only difference is that you cannot visibly see Him because

He is a Spirit.

> *"The grace of our Lord Jesus Christ, and the love of God, and the fellowship of the Holy Spirit be with you all Amen."* **- 2 Corinthians 13:14.**

6. PRAYING IN THE SPIRIT

Praying in tongues is empowered by the Holy Spirit to fulfill the purposes of God.

> *"For if I pray in tongues, my spirit prays, but my understanding is unfruitful. What is the conclusion then? I will pray with the spirit, and I will also pray with the understanding. I will sing with the spirit, and I will also sing with the understanding"* **- 1 Corinthians 14:14-15.**

7. WORSHIP IN THE SPIRIT

To worship the Lord in tongues is to worship in Spirit. This enables believers to glorify Jesus which gladdens the heart of the Father and our Lord Jesus. It also fosters an intimate relationship with the Lord **(1 Corinthians 14:14-15)**

Jesus said**,** *"but the hour is coming, and now is, when the true worshippers will worship the Father in Spirit and truth; for the Father is seeking such to worship Him. God is a Spirit and those who worship Him must worship in Spirit and truth"* **- John 4: 23-24.**

8. GROWING IN THE SPIRIT

Growing in the Spirit is achieved by constantly feeding your spirit with the word of God by studying, memorizing, meditating, and proclaiming God's word every day. You can also grow in the Spirit by exercising your spirit in prayer, worship, fellowship with other believers and walking with the Holy Spirit.

BLESSINGS OF INTERACTING WITH THE HOLY SPIRIT

These are the blessings received by interacting with the Holy Spirit
- The Holy Spirit will guide you to make godly decisions all the time as you depend on Him.
- He will reveal God's thoughts to you so that you will know the will of God in every situation.
- He would reveal the promises of God to you through the word of God and divine revelation.
- He will reveal the plans and purposes of God to you
- He will reveal all satanic plans against you and divine strategies to combat the devil and be victorious all the time.
- He will teach you the truth of God's word.
- He will endow you with power to overcome sin.
- Being spiritually minded will give you peace and life in abundance.
- He will empower you to live holy lifestyle.
- He will empower you to pray according to the will of God with an assurance of answers to prayers.
- He will expose deception, lies, tricks and schemes of satan to you; including impending dangers that you were not aware of.

QUESTIONS

1. Define the term baptism. What are the different types of baptism?
2. Read Romans 6:3-5 and explain the significance of water baptism and its importance in the life of every Believer.
3. If you were called upon to conduct water baptism for a new believer, how would you describe the process of water baptism and the blessings involved in the life of a Believer?
4. What is the Baptism of the Holy Spirit? Who is the baptizer in the Holy Spirit? List the steps to receiving the Baptism of the Holy Spirit?
5. Explain in your own words; who is the Holy Spirit? what are the works of the Holy Spirit? Why was He sent to the earth? Read John 16:13 and Isaiah 11:2.
6. Explain some of the practical ways of working with the Holy Spirit?
7. In Galatians 5:18, the scripture says " be led by the Holy Spirit" what do you understand by this?
8. In Romans 8:14, the word of God says: "because those who are led by the Holy Spirit are ---------- of ------------.
9. Romans 8:6 -8 says "The mind of sinful nature is ----------, but the mind controlled by the Spirit is ----------- and --------------. The sinful mind is ---------------- to God, it does not submit to God's law, nor can it do so. Those controlled by the sinful nature cannot please ----------"
10. I Corinthians 14:14 and John 4:23-24 mentioned these terms "Pray in the Spirit and Understanding; "Worship in Spirit and Truth" what do these terms mean? Explain

11. List some of the experiences you have had while interacting with the Holy Spirit? Give a brief testimony of how you have been led by the Holy Spirit in making certain decisions and the outcome.

CHAPTER 8

THE LAYING ON OF HANDS

AIM:
To teach the doctrine of laying on of hands.

OBJECTIVES:
At the end of the teaching, believers should be able to:
- Explain the definition of laying on of hands.
- Understand the purpose and blessings involved in laying on of hands.
- Heed the biblical warnings of hasty laying on of hands.

DOCTRINES OF LAYING ON OF HANDS

What is laying on of hands?

It is a spiritual act of laying hands on someone or thing for the purpose of consecration or impartation of blessings and anointing or to physically arrest someone.

PURPOSE AND BLESSINGS OF LAYING ON OF HANDS

These are some of the blessings and purposes of laying on of hands.
- To impart spiritual gifts to someone - 2nd Timothy 1:16.
- To release the anointing to heal those who are sick - Acts 9:17; Mark 16:16.
- For ordination into ministry as labourers in God's Vineyard - Acts 6:6; Acts 13:3.
- To release the Baptism of Holy Spirit on believers - Acts 8:7; 19:6.
- To impart the power and ability to prophesy on believers - 1st Tim 4:14.
- To free someone bound by demons, to live a fulfilling life - Mark 16:16; Acts 19:11-12.
- Impartation of anointing for a specific work of the Lord - 2 Kings 13:15-17.
- To consecrate an equipment to the service to the Lord.
- To raise a dead person - Mark 5:41; Acts 20:9-12.

EFFECTS OF LAYING ON OF HANDS IN THE OLD TESTAMENT

- Jacob laid hands on Ephraim instead of Manasseh to impart blessings - Genesis 48:14.
- Moses inaugurated Joshua as his successor by imparting an anointing for authority, wisdom and leadership.
- Moses elected leaders to assist him in his leadership role - Numbers 27:18-23; Deuteronomy 34:9.
- Moses prayed for 70 elders to assist him in his divine assignment.
- Elijah anointed Jehu as king and Elisha as a prophet as he laid his hands on them.
- Elisha imparted anointing for warfare on Joash the king of Israel - 2 Kings 13:15-17.

EFFECTS OF LAYING ON OF HANDS IN THE NEW TESTAMENT

- Certain prophets and teachers in the Church at Antioch laid hands on Barnabas and Saul to impart the anointing for the work of the ministry - Acts 13:1-3.

- The Apostles prayed and laid hands on Stephen, Phillip, Procorus, Nicanor, Timon, Parmenas and Nicolas for the anointing to serve - Acts 6: 5-7.
- Ananias laid his hands on Saul, as instructed by the Lord, and imparted the anointing on him. Saul received healing in his eyes, the baptism of the Holy Spirit and revelation of his ministry (the call of God) – Acts 9:17.
- Apostle Paul laid hands on Timothy to impart spiritual gifts - 2nd Timothy 1:6-7.
- The divine promise that believers will lay hands on the sick to release the anointing for healing is still evident in the body of Christ today - Mark 16:17-18.
- Timothy received a gift through a prophetic word given by the elders when they laid hands on him – 1 Timothy 4:14.
- Prayer and laying on of hands by Church elders with anointing oil will release the power to heal the sick – James 5:13-15.
- The authorities laid hands on Peter and John as they were arrested and jailed - Acts 4:1-4.
- Jesus took a dead 12 years old girl by the hand and said "little girl, I say to you arise" and she was raised to life - Mark 5:41.

WARNING AGAINST HASTY LAYING ON OF HANDS

Apostle Paul warned Timothy to never be hasty in laying hands on anyone, to avoid sharing their sins

1 Timothy 5:22 says *" Do not be hasty in the laying on of hands, and do not share in the sins of others. Keep yourself pure"*.

In other words, leaders should heed the warnings given by Apostle Paul before ordaining anyone into the office of a Deacon or Bishop (1 Timothy 3:1-13); they must first be tested in terms of character, with spiritual and moral integrity; marital status of monogamy, hospitable, self-controlled, have the ability to teach, not greedy for money, be able to lead their family in the ways of the Lord and have a good attitude towards unbelievers. They must not be recent converts in order to prevent pride. If they are women, they must be temperate, worthy of respect, trustworthy, have control over their tongues, must be under divine authority and be submissive to their husbands.

This instruction must be followed to prevent chaos in the Church and keep spiritual leaders accountable to God on how they manage the body of Christ, an assignment they will give account for on judgement day, hence the warning: "do not share in the sins of others".

There is a parallel of this doctrine in the spiritual realm; Just as the Lord uses His people to lay hands on one another to impart anointing, spiritual blessings, spiritual gifts, baptism of the Holy Spirit, healing, deliverance, raising of the dead e.t.c., the devil uses his agents to release evil spirits on people and objects to cause destruction, chaos, pain, sorrow and loss of blessings.

QUESTIONS

1. Define the term "Laying on of hands"?
2. List 7 purposes and blessings of laying on of hands?
3. In Genesis 48: 14, Jacob laid his hands and imparted blessings on ---- instead of ----
4. Moses inaugurated ------- by imparting the anointing for these purposes ----, -------------, ----
5. The apostles prayed and laid hands on Stephen, ----, Procorous, -----, Nicanor, ---, Timon for the anointing to —
6. In Mark 16:17-18 Jesus promised that believers would lay hands on the sick and they will -----
7. In James 5:13-15, what did God say the elders should do to those who are sick?
8. Read Acts 4:1-4 and explain what the authorities did to Peter and John
9. In Timothy 5:22, apostle Paul gave some warnings to Timothy, what are these warnings and the consequences of not heeding them?
10. Explain in your own words what Ananias did to Saul after his encounter with Jesus on the road to Damascus. List the effects and results of Ananias' obedience to the divine instructions and action on Saul.

CHAPTER 9

RESURRECTION OF THE DEAD

AIM:
To teach the dynamics of the resurrection of the dead

OBJECTIVES:
At the end of the teaching, believers should be able to:
- Explain the definition of Resurrection.
- Understand the physical and spiritual state of believers at death; in between death and resurrection.
- List the 2 different categories of resurrection and the nature of the resurrected body of believers.
- Apply **the divine instruction given to believers on how to raise the dead.**

THE DYNAMICS OF THE RESURRECTION OF THE DEAD
What is Resurrection?
(Greek: Anastasis) It is rising of the dead and restoration to life.
It is revival from disuse or inactivity or decay.

It is to be brought to life and to vigorous activity.

Apostle Paul gave the following explanation for the resurrection of the dead and the state of the resurrected bodies of believers.

> *"Now this I say, Brethren, that flesh and blood cannot inherit the kingdom of God; nor does corruption inherit incorruption. Behold, I tell you a mystery: We shall not all sleep, but we shall all be changed – in a moment, in the twinkling of an eye, at the last trumpet. For the trumpet will sound, and the dead will be raised incorruptible, and we shall be changed."* - **1 Corinthians 15:50-52.**

DYNAMICS OF RESURRECTION

THE RESURRECTION OF THE DEAD

The following scriptures explain the promises and assurance of the resurrection of believers from the dead and the purpose of Jesus' resurrection.

- Jesus is the resurrection and life - John 11:25.
- Jesus was raised from the dead for our JUSTIFICATION - Romans 4:25.
- The assurance of resurrection for Believers - 1 Thessalonians 4: 13-17.
- Jesus died, was buried and resurrected on the 3rd day - 1 Corinthians 15 3-8.
- God raised Jesus from the dead and loosed the pains of death - Acts 2:23-24.
- The promise of resurrection from the dead - 1 Corinthians 15:15.

STAGES OF RESURRECTION AFTER DEATH

These are the stages of how **God created man**, the state of man **when he dies,** the process of physical decay of the body; where the soul goes to await the judgement of God and what happens to the spirit of man after death.

> *"And God formed man out of the dust, breathed into his nostrils the breath of life."* - **Genesis 2:7.**

At death, the body of man decays and becomes dust (**Ecclesiastes 3:18-21**). This is the physical and spiritual state of believers' body at death; the body buried in the ground goes through the process of physical decay, then the soul goes to paradise awaiting the day of judgment and the human spirit returns to God. Jesus was raised from the tomb by the power of the Holy Spirit as the first fruit from the dead.

> *"The dust will return to the earth as it was, and the spirit will return to God who gave it."* - **Ecclesiastes 12:7.**

And finally, the dead will be raised to face judgement, the believer will be raised to eternal life and the unbeliever raised to eternal damnation – which is Hell...

STAGE BETWEEN DEATH AND RESURRECTION

This stage explains what happens to believers after death in comparison to the souls of those who rejected Christ (unbelievers).

The souls of believers will not be in Sheol after death, but in paradise until judgement day (Psalm 16:8-11).

Jesus said to the thief on the cross *"today you will be with Me in paradise -* Luke 23:43.

Since Jesus was raised from the dead, He became the first fruit of those who have died in the Lord (1Corinthians 15:20-22)

RESURRECTION FORETOLD IN THE OLD TESTAMENT

These biblical verses explain how resurrection was foretold in the Old Testament and later manifested in the New Testament.

Job said this: "*After my skin is destroyed, this I know, that in my flesh I shall see God*" **- Job 19: 25-27**.

Isaiah also mentioned that: "*Your dead shall live; together with my dead body they shall arise, awake and sing, you who dwell in the dust; for your dew is like the dew of herbs, and the earth shall cast out the dead*" - **Isaiah 26:19.**

Finally, Daniel said "*and many of those who sleep in the dust of the earth shall awake, some to everlasting life, some to shame and everlasting contempt*" - **Daniel 12:2.**

RESURRECTION MANIFESTED IN THE NEW TESTAMENT

Jesus confirmed the prophetic word uttered by Prophet Daniel, when said "*Do not marvel at this; for the hour is coming in which all who are in the grave will hear His voice, and come forth – those who have done good to the resurrection of life and those who have done evil, to the resurrection of condemnation*" **- John 5:28-29**.

This is what occurred immediately Jesus died on the Cross in the account of Matthew: "*And the graves were opened and many bodies of the saints who had fallen asleep were raised*" **- Matthew 27:52-53.**

Apostle Paul mentioned that, "*For if we believe that Jesus died and rose again, even so God will bring with Him those who sleep in Jesus*" **-** 1 **Thessalonians 4:14-18**

(For further study read: Revelation 20:4-6; Acts 1:11; I John 3:14)

THE NATURE OF A BELIEVER'S RESURRECTED BODY

The following scriptures describe the nature of a believer's resurrected body in heaven.

The bible describes the resurrected body of believers as being a real body with flesh and bones, but spiritual; it is a heavenly and glorious body which has been redeemed by the blood of Jesus. It will be an incorruptible body which cannot decay and will live forever – eternally.

The resurrected body of a believer will be:
- An incorruptible body - 1 Corinthians 15:42.
- A heavenly body - 1 Corinthians 15:47- 49; 2 Corinthians 5:1-6.
- A glorious body - Philippians 3:21; Luke 24:39.
- A redeemed body - 2 Corinthians 5:4; Romans 8:11-23.
- A spiritual body - 1 Corinthians 15:44.
- A real body with flesh and bones - 1 Corinthians 15:22; John 5:28; Revelation 20:12; Luke 24:39.

THESE ARE THE TWO CATEGORIES OF BIBLICAL RESURRECTION

(1) RESURRECTION OF THE RIGHTEOUS (BELIEVERS)
- The first resurrection - Revelation 20:4-6.
- The resurrection of the just - Luke 14:14; Acts 24:15.
- The resurrection of life - John 5:29.
- The awakening to everlasting life - Daniel 12:2.

(2) RESURRECTION OF THE UNRIGHTEOUS (UNBELIEVERS)
- The second resurrection - Revelation 20:4-6.
- The resurrection of the unjust - Acts 24:15.
- The resurrection of damnation - John 5:29.
- The awakening to shame and everlasting contempt - Daniel 12:2.
- The final state of the unredeemed is Hell. *Jesus said "fear Him who is able to destroy both body and soul in Hell"* - Matthew 10:28. (For further study read Daniel 7:11).

DIVINE INSTRUCTIONS TO RAISE THE DEAD
Jesus gave a divine instruction to believers: *"as you go preach this message: "the kingdom of heaven is near". Heal the sick, raise the dead..."* - **Matthew 10: 7-8.**

These scriptural verses confirm that Jesus raised the dead in His earthly ministry. His apostles also raised the dead by obeying instruction given by Jesus on how to raise the dead. This grace is also available to believers today.

- It is a divine Command to raise the dead as part of evangelism - Mark 16:17; Matthew 10:7-8.
- Jesus did not see death - Hebrews 11:5.
- Death is swallowed up - 1st Corinthians 15:54.
- Jesus raised the dead - Luke 7:11-17.
- Jesus raised Lazarus - John 11:28-44.
- The dead will hear the voice of Jesus and come to life - John 5:25-30.
- God gave life to the dead and calls those things that are not as if they were - Romans 8:14; Romans 4:17.
- Jesus has power over death - Hebrews 2:14.
- Peter raised Dorcas to life - Acts 9:36-42.
- Apostle Paul raised Eutychus to life - Acts 20:7-12.
- God's promise to redeem people from the power of the grave - Hosea 13:14.

QUESTIONS

1. What is the meaning of resurrection?
2. After reading 1st Corinthians 15:15, do you believe that believers will be resurrected some day? What is the implication of this statement in contrast to the non – Christian beliefs of re – incarnation? Explain your answer.
3. Name 3 ways the bible describes the resurrected body of believers after death?
4. What happens to a believers' body at death?
5. What do you believe happens to the believers' soul and spirit between the period of death and the period of resurrection from the dead? Support your answers with biblical verses.
6. List 2 categories of resurrection mentioned in the bible and explain with the appropriate scriptures.
7. Search through the bible and cite several occasions where Jesus raised the dead.
9. Relate these occasions to when the apostles obeyed the divine command from the lord to raise the dead (Acts 9:36-42; Acts 20:7-12). They succeeded in accomplishing it, do you think the same power and authority to raise the dead is available for believers today? Support your answer with practical experience and with the scriptures.
10. Read Matthew 10:7-8 and explain the command Jesus gave to every Believer to raise the dead whenever they are confronted with this situation. Have you personally prayed for the dead to come to life?

Have you observed it before in other ministries or Churches?

11. If you believe the scriptural passage in Hebrews 9:27 which says that "it is appointed for man to die once, and after that judgement", what should be your attitude to life here on earth, in terms of how you relate to other people, your attitude towards accumulation of wealth and money, and the quality of service that you are giving to the work of the Lord?

CHAPTER 10

ETERNAL JUDGEMENT AND REWARDS

AIM:
To teach the dynamics and process of eternal judgement and rewards.

OBJECTIVES:
At the end of the teaching, believers should be able to:
- Identify the 2 categories of rewards and have clarity on how these rewards will be given to believers.
- Describe the dynamics of God's judgment.
- Apply the steps believers need to take to achieve perfection and the roles of believers in heaven

SECTION A

What is a Reward?
It is a return or recompense for service or merit; it is a requital for good or evil.

Note that rewards will be given to believers who identify their specific calling, obey the call of God and stay faithful in fulfilling it.

We will be judged on how we obeyed Godly authorities, our Character – how we build our own individual lives, the motives of our hearts whilst serving the Lord and how we related to other people on earth, including believers and Non - believers.

In Matthew 19:29, Jesus encouraged His disciples when Peter was concerned about his salvation and the possibility of making it to heaven. He said, "And everyone who has left house, or brother, or sister, or father, or mother, or wife, or children, or lands for my names' sake, shall receive a hundredfold, and inherit eternal life"

However, there are 2 categories of rewards, namely: Earthly & Heavenly Rewards.

UNDERSTANDING EARTHLY AND HEAVENLY REWARDS

In this section we will be dealing with the biblical understanding of these rewards and how they will be given to believers. These result from utilization of developed ministry and spiritual gifts with fruitful outcomes.

DYNAMICS OF REWARDS

"You will only observe with your eyes and see the punishment of the wicked" **- Psalm 91:8**.

"See the Sovereign Lord comes with power… see His reward is with Him, and His recompense accompanies Him" **- Isaiah 40:10**.

Hosea 4:9 - *"It will be like people, like Priests. The Lord will punish both of them for their ways and repay them for their deeds"*.

Revelation 22:12 - *"Behold, I Am coming soon! My reward is with Me and I will give to everyone according to what he has done."*

Matthew 5:11-12 - *"Due to persecution endured on earth, the Lord will give you an heavenly reward"*

Matthew 6:1-4 - *"When you give to the poor discretely, the Lord will reward you"*

Luke 6:35 - *"The Lord said "…love your enemies, do good to them, lend without expectation of returns and the Lord will reward you greatly".*

Luke 23:41- *"The Lord promised the reward of repentance of sins (read about the criminal on the cross beside Jesus").*

I Corinthians 3:8-15 - *"The man who plants and the one who waters will be rewarded each according to his own labour".*

Colossians 2:18 – *"This is a warning about the deception in the last days with the consequence of losing your reward if you fall. "Do not let anyone who delights in false humility and worship of angels disqualify you for the prize"*

Hebrews 11:26 - *"Moses rejected the wealth and opulence of Pharaoh's house for the sake of Christ's greater value and looked ahead to his reward".*

2 John 8 - *"(Be alert!)-watch out! This is a warning that deception in the last days could cause you to lose your reward"*

EARTHLY REWARDS

When Peter was concerned about the sacrifices he made for his salvation, Jesus encouraged His disciples with these words in Matthew 19:29. He said, "And everyone who has left house, or brother, or sister, or father, or mother, or wife, or children, or lands for my names' sake, shall receive a hundredfold, and inherit eternal life." This is also a confirmation that there are earthly rewards and heavenly rewards.

In Matthew 25:19-30, Jesus gave a parable to reassure believers of their rewards if they are faithful to the assignments God gave them.

"AFTER A LONG TIME THE LORD OF THOSE SERVANTS CAME TO SETTLE ACCOUNT WITH THEM"

This signifies our Lord Jesus' second coming to judge the saints. It also signifies that the day of accountability is guaranteed and as sure as death.

He further stressed that *"many are Called, but few are chosen ..."* (the few represents those who obeyed, endured the trials, obstacles, testing, and persecution while fulfilling their divine assignment).

CATEGORIES OF EARTHLY REWARDS

PROPHET & THE RIGHTEOUS MAN
Jesus said, *"Anyone who receives a Prophet because he is a Prophet will receive a Prophet's reward and anyone who receives a righteous man because he is a righteous man will receive a righteous man's reward."* - Matthew 10:41-42.

PERSISTENCE IN FAITHFULLY SERVING GOD
Apostle Paul further encourages believers in 1st Corinthians 15:58, *"Therefore my dear brothers, stand firm. Let nothing move you. Always give yourself fully to the work of the Lord, because you know that your labor in the Lord is not in vain"*.

PRODUCTIVENESS IN SERVING GOD
Jesus stressed this information to His disciples, *"You did not choose me, but I chose you to go and appointed you to go and bear fruit, the fruit that will last....."* **John 15:16-17.** This also highlights that rewards follow fruits that grow as a result of serving the Lord.

DIVINE HONOUR IN SERVING GOD
Jesus further affirmed through His word, the promise of divine honor guaranteed for believers who serve Him and make it to heaven;: *"Whoever*

serves me must follow me; and where I am, my servants also will be. My father will honor the one who serves Me" **- John 12:26.**

ASSURANCE OF REWARDS IN SERVING GOD

Finally, Jesus said *"And behold I am coming quickly, and My reward is with Me, to give to everyone according to his work"* - **Revelation 22:12.**

REWARD OF HARVEST FOR SEEDS SOWN

The word of God in Genesis 8:22 declares *"as the earth remains, ….seedtime and harvest shall never cease….."*

As you sow financial seeds into ministries to propagate the Kingdom of God, the Lord would release a harvest of blessings into your life.

The scripture declares that "a gift opens the way for the giver and ushers him into the presence of the great. (Proverbs 18:16) Examples of the manifestation of this scripture is in the lives of Daniel, Joseph and others

HEAVENLY REWARDS

THESE ARE THE DIFFERENT REWARDS THE LORD HAS PROMISED TO GIVE BELIEVERS WHO ENDURE TO THE END. Jesus said, *"I am coming soon; hold on to what you have, so that no one will take your Crown."* - **Revelation 3:11.**

The Lord will reward believers according to their faithfulness in fulfilling the divine assignment given to them. As he said to the man who multiplied the 5 talents given to him and gained extra 5 talents due to his diligence and productiveness, he will say the same to faithful believers who use their talents to glorify him on earth. *"Well done, good and faithful servant, you were faithful over a few things. I will make you ruler over many things. Enter into the joy of your Lord"* **- Matthew 25:21.**

Lamentation 5:16 is a warning to those who will lose their rewards due to sin in their lives.

The following is an exposition of the different types of rewards awaiting believers in Heaven as a result of ministry works carried out here on earth.

CROWN OF GLORY

This is the reward for spiritual leaders who care for the flock (Church members) willingly, out of love and honestly by being good examples and with respect. **- I Peter 5:2-4.**

> *"Therefore my beloved and longed for Brethren, my joy and Crown…"* **- Philippians 4:1.**

CROWN OF REJOICING

This is the promised reward for spiritual leaders who have been diligent in caring for the spiritual wellbeing of Jesus' sheep to present them blameless before the Lord **- 1 Thessalonians 2:19-20.**

CROWN OF LIFE

Jesus said, *"…Be **faithful** till death and I will give the crown of life"*. - **Revelation 2:10**.

James said, *"Blessed is the man who **endures temptation**, for when he has been **approved**, he will receive the **crown of life** which the Lord has promised to those who love Him"* **- James 1:12**.

CROWN OF RIGHTEOUSNESS

After exhorting Timothy, Apostle Paul gave his own valedictory speech and mentioned that, as a result of his **ministry and every mission accomplished with excellence;** he was looking forward to the promise of the crown of righteousness as a reward promised to all believers by our Lord and Savior Jesus.

> *"Finally, there is in store for me the crown of righteousness, which the Lord, the righteous judge,*

will award to me on that day – and not only to me, but also to all who have longed for His appearing" - **2 Timothy 4:8,**

INCORRUPTIBLE CROWN

Apostle Paul, further encouraged all believers to run the race(fulfilling their divine assignment) by exercising self-control, discipline, be well focused, i.e. looking ahead without distraction in order to win the price (reward of the incorruptible crown)

> *"And anyone who competes for a prize is temperate (exercises self-control) in all things. Now they do it to obtain a perishable crown, but we for an imperishable crown. Therefore, I run thus: not with uncertainty. Thus, I fight: not as one who beats the air. But I discipline my body and bring it into subjection, lest, when I have preached to others, I myself should become disqualified."* - **1 Corinthians 9:25-27.**

GOD'S SAINTS AND SERVANTS

> *"...And that you should reward your servants the prophets and the saints and those who fear your name, small and great. And should destroy those who destroy the earth."* - **Revelation 11:18.**

CROWNS OF GOLD

> *"Surrounding the throne were twenty four other thrones, and seated on them were twenty four elders. They were dressed in whites and had crowns of Gold on their heads."* - **Revelation 4:4.**

These are biblical explanations for the rewards Jesus promised Believers.

Apostle Paul admonished believers that: *"God is not unjust; He will not forget your work and the love you have shown Him as you have helped His people and continue to help them…… we do not want you to become lazy but to imitate those who through faith and patience inherit what has been promised"* - **Hebrews 6:10-12.**

Jesus said "When the Son of man comes in His Glory, and all the angels with Him, He will sit on His throne in heavenly Glory. All the nations will be gathered before Him, and He will separate the people one from another as a shepherd separates the sheep (believers who obeyed and fulfilled their calling and bore fruits) from the goats (unbelievers who rejected Jesus). He will put the sheep on His right and the goats on his left……"

> *"Then he will say to those on His left, 'depart from Me, you who are cursed, into eternal fire prepared for the devil and his angels"* - **Matthew 25: 31- 46.**

> *"Behold I am coming soon! My reward is with Me, and I will give to everyone according to what he has done"* - **Revelation 22:12.**

> *"**And** I saw the dead, great and small, standing before the **throne,** and books were opened. Another **book was opened,** which is **the book of life**. The dead were judged according to what they had done as recorded in the books. The sea gave up the dead that were in it, and death and Hades gave up the dead that were in them, and each person was judged according to what he had done. Then death and Hades were thrown into the Lake of fire. The lake of fire is the second death. If anyone's name was not found written in the book of life, he was thrown into the lake of fire"* - **Revelation 20:12.**

HEAVENLY INHERITANCE – BLESSINGS AND DIVINE PROMISE FOR OVERCOMERS

This is a summary of the promises Jesus gave to believers who overcome and make it to heaven.

- The right to eat of the tree of life & a gift of the crown of life which no one else can take away from you - Revelation 2:10; Revelation 2:7.
- Escape from being hurt by the second death - Revelation 20:6.
- They will receive some of the hidden manna to eat and white stones with a new name (only known by the owner) written on it - Revelation 2:17.
- Authority to rule over nations and a gift of the morning star - Revelation 2:26 & Revelation 2:28.
- A gift of white linen - (Righteous act of the Saints) - Revelation 3:5.
- Their names will be permanently placed in the lamb's book of life - Luke 10:20. You will be made permanent pillars in the temple of God and will have the names of God, the new Jerusalem and the new name of Jesus written on you - Revelation 3:12.
- The right (privilege) to sit with Jesus on His throne - Revelation 3:21.
- The honour to eat and drink at Jesus' table in His kingdom.
- A place to sit on the thrones to judge the twelve tribes of Israel, nations as an inheritance and the ends of the earth for possession – Psalm 2:8 ; Luke 22:30
- A place at the wedding supper of the Lamb - Revelation 19:9.
- A drink from the river of life - Revelation 21:6.

SECTION B
ETERNAL JUDGEMENT

What is ETERNAL JUDGEMENT?
It is the period of accountability for all human race after death where everyone will stand before the judgement seat of Jesus Christ to give an account of their lives on earth; whether they received Christ as Lord and

fulfilled their purpose on earth, or not. While some will receive eternal life others will receive eternal judgement of CONDEMNATION).

The scriptures make it clear that there is a book in heaven where Angels record the activities of each human being on earth.

> *"And I saw the dead, great and small, standing before the throne, and <u>books were opened. Another book</u> was opened, <u>which is the Book of life</u>. The dead were judged according to what they had done as recorded in the books ... if anyone's name was not found written in the book of life, he was thrown into the lake of fire"* - **Revelation 20: 12-14.**

The word of God clearly says: *"It is appointed for men to die once, after this judgement"* - **Hebrews 9:27**.

The bible also says, *"for we shall all stand before the judgement seat of Christ that each one may receive what is due him for the things done while in the body, whether good or bad."* - **2nd Corinthians 5:10**.

> *"you, then, why do you judge your brother ... for we will all stand before the judgement seat ... so then, each of us will give an account of himself to God"* - **Romans 14:10.**

The scripture confirmed this statement about Jesus that, *"And has given Him authority to execute judgement also, because he is the Son of man. Do not marvel at this; for the hour is coming in which all who are in the graves will hear His voice, and come forth – those who have done good, to the resurrection of life and those who have done evil, to the resurrection of condemnation."* - **John 5: 27-29.**

> *"God will give to each person according to what he has done. To those who by **persistence** in **doing good seek glory, honor and immortality, He will***

*give eternal life. But for those who are **self - seeking and who reject the truth and follow evil**, there will be wrath and anger. There will be trouble and distress for every human being who does evil: first for the Jew, then for the Gentile; **but glory, honor and peace for everyone who does good**. First for the Jew, then for the Gentile. For God does not show favoritism."* - **Romans 2:6-11.**

DYNAMICS OF JUDGEMENT OF GOD
ETERNAL JUDGEMENT

The judgment of God on unbelievers

Daniel said: *"I watched till thrones were put in place, and the Ancient of Days was seated; His garment was white as snow, and the hair of His head was like pure wool. His throne was a fiery flame, its wheels a burning fire; a fiery stream issued and came forth from before Him. A thousand thousands ministered to Him. Ten thousand times ten thousand stood before Him. The court was seated, and the **books** were opened."* **Daniel 7:9 -10.**

Apostle Paul said, "… and to give you who are troubled rest with us, when the Lord Jesus is revealed from heaven with His mighty angels, in flaming fire taking vengeance on those who do not know God, and on those who do not obey the gospel of our Lord Jesus Christ. These will be punished with everlasting destruction from the presence of the Lord and from the glory of His power." - **2 Thessalonians 1:7b-9.**

(For further study: John 5:22-27; Acts 17:31)

CATEGORIES OF THE JUDGEMENT OF GOD

The word of God declares that, "for the time has come for judgment to begin at the house of God, and if it begins with us first, what will be the end of those who do not obey the gospel of God" **- I Peter 4:17.**

These are the three categories of the judgment of God.

1. The judgment of believers through the word of God, revelation/ knowledge of God and fruits from the deployment of the call of God on your life (ministry and spiritual gifts) - **Matthew 11:20-24; Luke 12:48.**
2. The judgment of unbelievers will be carried out through God's creation based on opportunities presented to unbelievers to hear the gospel at least once. **(Romans 1:20 ; John 12:47-48)** and those who never had the chance to hear the gospel of Jesus.
3. The judgment of Jews will be carried out by Jesus through the laws of Moses - **Romans 2:12; Matthew 19:28.**

SECTION C
PRINCIPLES AND STANDARDS OF THE JUDGEMENT OF GOD

These are the principles and standards the Lord will use to judge both believers and unbelievers according to their deeds on earth.

- People will be judged according to the opportunities presented to them to hear the gospel of Jesus - Matthew 11:21-24; Luke 12:28.
- People will be judged by Jesus who has the records of men's activities on earth - Ecclesiastes 12:14; Revelation 20:12.
- People will be judged according to their attitude towards Jesus - Jude 15; John 12:48; Luke 12:8-9.
- People will be judged with righteous judgement - Acts 17:31; Psalm 96:13.
- People will be judged according to Holy standards - Romans 2:6-11; Revelation 22:12.
- Rewards and punishments will be in different degrees - Luke 19:16-19; Luke 12:47-48.
- People will be judged according to the words uttered from their mouth; whether good or bad - Matthew 12: 36-37.
- People will be judged according to their stewardship of the earth -

Genesis 1:26-30.

SECTION D
PURPOSE OF JUDGEMENT AND REWARDS

These are the purposes of God's judgment and rewards on human beings:
- To determine the quality of everyone's work on earth - 1st Corinthians 3:13.
- To declare the righteous judgement of God - Revelation 19:1-2.
- To punish those who did evil or reward those who fulfilled God's purpose on earth - Matthew 16:27; Romans 2:6-9; Revelation 22:12.
- To reveal and reward the motive of everyone's heart and character while serving the Lord on earth - 1 Corinthians 4:5.

CLASSES OF PEOPLE TO BE JUDGED

Jesus used metaphors to describe the classes of men that will stand before the judgment seat of Christ.
- The Sheep and Goats - Matthew 25:33.
- The Just and the Wicked - Matthew 13:49.
- The Saints and the Unrighteous - 2 Thessalonians 1:8-10.

Among these classes of people, some will be eternally blessed and others will be eternally cursed - Matthew 25:34, 41.

The final destination of man will either be heaven or hell! There is no grey area between these two states of existence.

THE INHERITANCE & ROLE OF BELIEVERS IN HEAVEN

The bible explains the process of inheritance for believers and the roles believers will play in heaven in these scriptures;

> *"to an inheritance incorruptible and undefiled and that does not fade away, reserved in heaven for you"*- **I Peter 1:4.**
>
> *"He who overcomes shall inherit all things, and I will be his God and he shall be my son"* - **Revelation 21:7.**

These are the inheritance and roles believers will play in Heaven;
- Believers who overcome will be given the responsibility to judge the world and to judge angels - 1st Corinthians 6:2-3.
- Believers will have food to eat in heaven - Revelation 2:7; Luke 22:30.
- Every believer will live in a mansion - John 14:2.
- Every believer will be given a specific seat at the banquet table and different types of crowns will be given as rewards - Revelation 3:11.
- Believers will be given linen clothes to wear - Revelation 19:8.
- Believers will live in a perpetual state of peace and divine health, where there will be no more tears or pain - Revelation 21:4.
- Books in Heaven that chronicle the lives of believers fulfilling the call of God, their character and utilization of ministry and spiritual gifts, will be opened on the day of Judgment - Revelation 20: 12-13; 22:12.
- Believers whose names are written in the BOOK OF LIFE will be given new names - Luke 10: 20; Revelation 3:5; Revelation 2:17.

THE CHARACTERISTICS OF THOSE WHO WILL NOT INHERIT THE KINGDOM OF GOD

The Lord identified different characteristics and categories of people who will not inherit the Kingdom of God, if they fail to repent and turn away from wickedness.

"But the cowardly, unbelieving, abominable, murderers, sexually immoral, sorcerers, idolaters, and all liars shall have their part in the lake which burns with fire and brimstone, which is the second death" - **Revelation 21:8.**

"But these shall by no means enter it anything that defiles, or causes an abomination or a lie but only those who are written in the Lamb's Book of Life." - **Revelation 21:27.**

"But outside are the dogs and sorcerers and sexually immoral and murderers and idolaters and whoever loves and practice a lie." - **Revelation 22:15.**

QUESTIONS

- Define the term "Reward"?
- How many categories of rewards did Jesus promise those who performed the assignment given to them well here on earth? Name these categories.
- Read this word of encouragement from Apostle Paul in I Corinthians 15:58 "Therefore my dear brothers, ------------ ------. Let nothing move you. Always give yourself fully to the ------ of the Lord, because you know that your ------------- in the Lord is not in ------
- In John 12:26, what did Jesus promise those who serve Him?
- The verse in Revelation 22:12 explain the rewards Jesus would be giving to everyone upon His return. Have you found out your specific calling,

your purpose here on earth, the Divine assignment prepared for you by God in advance (Ephesians 2:10). If so, are you fulfilling it? Make a list of these assignments. If Jesus were to ask you to give an account of this work, what would you show Him?
- In Revelation 20:12-14, what do you understand by the term "Books were opened" on the day of judgement?
- When the dead, great and small stand before the throne of God to be judged, "another book was opened" what is the purpose of this book?
- What is the book of life? And what happens to those whose names were not found in it?

CHAPTER 11

FULL ASSURANCE OF SALVATION FOR NEW BELIEVERS

Aim:
- To teach and assure new believers of their salvation experience.
- To teach believers how to avoid the arrows of doubt and deception that may cause them to backslide and doubt their salvation experience.

Objective:
At the end of the teaching, new Believers should:
- Have a better understanding and assurance of their salvation and be able to stand firm in the face of persecution, affliction, testing, trials and trouble.
- Understand the factors that can hinder a full experience of the assurance of salvation.
- Have enough confidence to carry out exercises on the full assurance of salvation and answer relevant questions

Jesus said: *"these things I have spoken to you, that in me you may have peace. In the world you will have tribulation; but be of good cheer, I have overcome the world"* - **John 16:33**.

SECTION A

The different categories of assurance are;
- Assurance of hope (Hebrews 6:10-12)
- Assurance of faith (Hebrews 10:22-23)
- Assurance of understanding (Colossians 2:2-3)
- Assurance of resurrection (1st Thessalonians 4:13-18; 2nd Corinthians 5:1-2)
- Assurance of eternity after death (I Corinthians 15:50-58)
- Assurance of salvation

For the purpose of this teaching, we will be dealing with the full assurance of salvation; factors which could hinder a believer from experiencing this assurance, how to prevent these hindrances and questions to be answered for a better understanding.

What is the Assurance of Salvation?
It is the state of being sure, certain, doubtless and confident that your sins are forgiven and you are accepted as a child of God. -John 1:12-13

HOW TO EXPERIENCE A FULL ASSURANCE OF SALVATION

For believers to experience a full assurance of salvation, it is important to do the following;
- Repent of all known sins before the Lord and receive forgiveness.
- Apply the faith you used to receive salvation to everyday living.
- Open your heart to receive the unconditional love and kindness of God.
- Fully obey the divine instructions and prophetic words written in God's word.

- Avoid being unequally yoked with unbelievers.
- Do not give satan a foothold in your life through persistent sins
- Spend quality time worshipping in God's presence.
- Spend quality time in prayers and in submission to the Holy Spirit.

These are factors which could hinder a believer from experiencing the full assurance of salvation.
- Unbelief - Mark 11:22-24.
- Inability to accept the love of God - 1st John 3:1.
- Unrepented sins - Hebrews 10:25.
- Disobedience to godly Instructions and His word - Acts 5:29-32; Hebrews 5:8-9.
- Being unequally yoked with unbelievers - James 4:4; I John 2:15-17)
- Giving satan a foothold (opening the door) in your life - James 4:7.
- Having an unforgiving heart - Mark 11:25.
- Grieving the Holy Spirit - Ephesians 4:30-31.
- Prayerlessness and spiritual slumber.
- Lack of being in the presence of God in worship - Revelation 2:4.

SECTION B
THE FULL ASSURANCE OF SALVATION

This section will help new believers stand firm in the face of satan's torment and persecutions or when the Christian journey becomes rough. It will serve as an anchor for your salvation or encouragement to stop you from backsliding.

Depending on the Holy Spirit and the word of God are the keys to having this assurance. The scriptures declare that: *"The Spirit Himself bears witness with our spirit that we are God's children.* (Romans 8:16). It further affirms that: *"These things I have written to you who believe (Believers) in the name of the Son of God, that you may know that you have eternal life, and that you may continue to believe in the name of the Son of God"* - I John 5:13

In other words, when you give your life to Jesus the next important step is for you to be assured of your salvation. There are 3 problem areas that can cause you to doubt your salvation, namely: satan attacks your mind with doubt, your own feelings or emotions and finally negative situations and circumstances surrounding you.

It is vital to understand that salvation is a spiritual experience and not natural; hence, to have victory over all these obstacles, you cannot rely on your feelings because it is like a yo-yo (rise today and fall tomorrow) and is driven by circumstances. You must depend fully on the Holy Spirit for help. Also the following exercises taken from the word of God will assist you in being fully assured of your salvation.

EXERCISES ON GETTING THE FULL ASSURANCE OF SALVATION

Therefore if anyone is in Christ, he is a new creation, the old has gone 1st Peter 4:1-5, and the new has come (abundant life in Christ Jesus – John 10:10. All this is from GOD, who reconciled us to Himself through Christ and has given us the ministry of reconciliation... 2nd Corinthians 5:17. Every new believer's faith and salvation will be tested by the devil; the above scripture is best for quoting when the devil comes to test you.

QUESTIONS

- What does the term "in Christ" mean?
- "If anyone is in Christ Jesus" signifies a conditional statement and can only be fulfilled by answering these questions; are you born again, baptized in the Holy Spirit and baptized in water?
  Read 1 Peter 1:18-23; Colossians 3:1-17; Ephesians 4:17-32; Ephesians 5:1-21 to help you answer the following question.
- What are the characteristics of the old nature (past lifestyle)? List some of

- the old habits and attitudes you used to have.
- What are the attributes of the new nature (new life in Christ Jesus)?
- List the new attributes you now possess to show your progress since becoming a believer?
- Who makes this occurrence (new habits and attitude) possible?
- What does the statement "reconciled us to Himself" mean?
- What is the ministry of reconciliation?
- Through whom has God reconciled us to Himself? How will the attributes of the "new man – new creation" help you through your spiritual journey in the kingdom of God?

(2) *"For it is by grace you have been saved, through faith and this is not from yourselves, it is the gift of God, not by works, so that no one can boast. For we are God's workmanship, created in Christ Jesus to do good works, which God prepared in advance for us to do"* **- Ephesians 2:8-10**

QUESTIONS

- What does this statement - you have been saved" mean to you?
- How were you saved?
- Understanding that you were not saved by works, identify several acts/works religious people believe they can do to reach God?
- What do you understand by grace?
- What do you understand by faith?
- What do you understand by the term "God's workmanship, created in Christ Jesus for good works"
- What are these good works? **- Ephesians 4:1-16.**

(3) *"… So you are no longer a slave, but a son; and since you are a son, God has made you also an heir."* **- Galatians 4:3-7**

QUESTIONS

- When were you a slave?
- What are the characteristics of a slave?
- How did you become a son and what do you understand by being a son?
- What are the rights and privileges of a son? Read John 1:13.
- Who is an heir of God?
- Through whom did you become an heir?
- List some of the blessings you inherited as an heir?

(4) *" But these are written that you may believe that Jesus is the Christ, the son of God, and that by believing you may have life in His name"* - **John 20:31**

QUESTIONS

- What was written that you may believe?
- Explain how you have life?
- What group of people are entitled to this life?
- What does it mean to believe? Read Romans 10:9-10.
- What does it mean to have life in Jesus' name?
- Comment on what the scripture says about the name of Jesus – Read Philippians 2:9.
- What type of life is the word of God referring to? - John 10:10 and 1st John 5: 11-13.

(5) "Yet to all who received him, to those who believed in His name, he gave the right to become children of God, children not born of natural descent, nor of human decision or a husband's will, but born of God" - **John 1:12**

QUESTIONS

- What does is it mean "to receive Him?" Who is this passage referring to?
- What is the difference between believing and receiving? - Romans 10:8-10.
- Explain the term "the right to become children of God?"
- Identify the difference between natural descent and being born of God?
- What does it mean to be born of God?
- Explain the steps needed to be born spiritually. Provide biblical verses for your answer.
- Explain the outcome of those people who refuse to receive Him?

(6) *"For you did not receive a spirit that makes you a slave again to fear, but you received the Spirit of Sonship and by Him we cry "Abba Father". The Spirit Himself testifies with our spirit that we are God's children. Now if we are God's children, then we are heirs – heirs of God and co-heirs with Christ, if indeed we share in His sufferings in order that we may also share in His Glory."* - **Romans 8:15-17**

QUESTIONS

- Comment on the term - "a spirit that makes you a slave again to fear..."
- What is the Spirit of Sonship?
- Who testifies with our spirit that we are God's children?
- Explain what it means to share in His sufferings?
- What does it mean to share in Jesus' glory?
- How does the Holy Spirit give the assurance of salvation to believers?
- If you are co-heirs with Christ, what is the promised inheritance?

(7) "And this is the testimony: God has given us eternal life, and this life is in His Son. He who has the Son has life; he who does not have the Son of God does not have life" - **I John 5: 11-13**

QUESTIONS

- Explain the term "Eternal life"
- What is a testimony?
- List some of the benefits of eternal life.
- What is the final state or outcome of anyone who rejects the invitation of salvation from the Son of God?
- How will Jesus react to such people on the day of judgement?
- Fill in the following gaps: "The ------------- has come to -----------------, to --------------- and to ---------------------; I am come to give ------------ and to give it ------------ John 10:10
- Who are the people God gave eternal life? List some of the characters expected from these group of people.

(8) *"For Christ died for sin once and for all, the righteous for the unrighteous, to bring you to God. He was put to death in the body, but made alive by the Spirit"* — **1 Peter 3:18**

QUESTIONS

- What does "Christ died for sins once and for all " mean? Read 1st John 1:7.
- What was used to pay the penalty of these sins?
- Explain the term "righteous for the unrighteous"? Read 2nd Corinthians 5:21 to help with the answer.
- Define the term "righteousness"?
- How did Jesus bring us to God?
- How was Jesus put to death in the body?
- Who made Jesus alive?
- Explain the process by which He was made alive?
- What is the term "Resurrection"?
- Suppose Jesus did not resurrect, what would have happened to our salvation? What about the hope of resurrection?

(9) *"But God demonstrates His own love toward us, in that while we were still sinners, Christ died for us. Much more then, having now been justified by His blood, we shall be saved from wrath through Him. For if when we were enemies we were reconciled to God through the death of His Son, much more, having been reconciled, we shall be saved by His life. And not only that, but we also rejoiced in God through our Lord Jesus Christ, through whom we have now received the reconciliation"* - **Romans 5:8-11**

QUESTIONS

- What is the love of God? Read 1 Corinthians 13:1-8 and list about 6 attributes of love mentioned in this passage of the word of God?
- Can God's love be compare to (the love of parents to children; love of husband to wife; platonic love which emanates from friendship? List the contrast (differences) that you can deduce from 1 Corinthians 13:1-8?
- What is justification? With what were you justified?
- What is reconciliation? How were you reconciled to God?
- What should be the expression and attitude of your heart towards God, knowing that he showed His love for you while you rejected Him?

(10) *"What then, shall we say in response to this? If God is for us, who can be against us? He who did not spare His Son, but gave Him up for us all – how will he not also, along with Him, graciously give us all things"* - **Romans 8:31-32**

"No, in all these things, we are more than conquerors through Him who loved us. For I am convinced that neither death, nor life, nor angels, nor demons, neither the present nor the future, nor any powers, neither height nor depth, nor anything else in all creation will be able to separate us from the love of God that is in Christ Jesus our Lord" - **Romans 8: 37-39**

QUESTIONS

- What do you understand by the statement "What then, shall we say in response to this?"
- With the knowledge of God sacrificed His only Son because of how much He loves and cares for us, how will you show gratitude to Him?
- The scripture says that "how will he not also, along with Him, graciously give us all things". Does this passage increase your expectation of answers to your prayers to God? If yes, explain how.
- If you are more than a conqueror through God who loves us, are you having victory daily in your Christian walk? If yes, list victorious experiences you have had recently and if no why do you think you are not experiencing victory?
- Fill in the gaps: "For I am convinced that neither ----------, nor -----------, nor --------, nor ------------, neither the present nor the future, nor any powers, neither height nor depth, nor anything else in all ------------ will be able to separate us from the ---------- of God that is in Christ Jesus our Lord.

SECTION C

This section explains the meaning of perfection and the divine grace given to man to attain perfection (spiritual maturity) with biblical guidelines. While Jesus was on earth, He attained this level of perfection and has set an example for us to emulate.

The bible declares that, *"Now let us move on to perfection, not laying again the foundation of repentance…."* **- Hebrews 6:1.**

PERFECTION (MATURITY)

What is Perfection?

Perfection (Greek: teleloo - which means perfected) means to be whole without fault or defect. To bring something to a successful conclusion or completion. To attain spiritual maturity, the position of a full grown son.

> *"... but the word of the oath, which came after the law, appoints the Son (Jesus) who has been perfected."* - **Hebrews 7:28b.**

> *"... but whoever keeps His word truly the love of God is perfected in him. By this we know that we are in Him."* **- I John 2:5.**

DIVINE GRACE FOR BELIEVERS TO ATTAIN PERFECTION

The word of God explains the process of divine grace given for man to attain perfection as follows: through the body of Jesus Christ and the blood of the new covenant; through the word of God; through faith and obedience & love; through the glory of the Lord; through the manifestation of the 5-fold ministries and finally through trials and testing,

1. **THROUGH JESUS BY THE BODY AND THE BLOOD OF THE NEW COVENANT**

    "For by one offering he has perfected forever those who are being sanctified" **- Hebrews 19:14.**

    (For further study, read Hebrews 7:11; 12:2; 13:20-21)

2. **THROUGH THE WORD OF GOD**

*"All scripture was given by inspiration of God and is profitable for doctrine, for reproof, for correction, for instruction in righteousness, that the man of God may be **complete**, thoroughly equipped for every good work"* **- 2 Timothy 3:16-17.**

3. **THROUGH FAITH, OBEDIENCE & LOVE**

"Love has been perfected in us in this…but perfect love casts out fear …but he who fears has not been made perfect in love" **- I John 4:17-18.**

"Was not Abraham our Father justified by works…? do you see faith was working together with his works, and by works faith was made perfect?" **- James 2:21-22**

4. **THROUGH THE GLORY OF THE LORD**

Jesus prayed to God the Father, *"And the glory which you gave me I have given them… I in them and you in Me; that they may be made **perfect** in one …"* **- John 17:22 -23**

5. **THROUGH THE 5-FOLD MINISTRIES OPERATING IN THE CHURCH**

*"And he himself gave some to be Apostles, some Prophets, some Evangelists, some Pastors and Teachers, for equipping of the saints… till we all come to the unity of the faith and of the knowledge of the son of God, to a **perfect man**, to the measure of stature of Christ"* **- Ephesians 4:11-13.**

6. **THROUGH TRIALS**

"My Brethren, count it all joy, when you fall into

*various trials, knowing that the testing of your faith produces patience. But let patience have its **perfect work**, that you may be **perfect and complete**, lacking nothing"* - **James 1:2-4**

7. **THROUGH TESTING**

   "I will bring the one-third through the fire, will refine them as silver is refined, and test them as gold is tested. They will call on My name, and I will answer them. I will say, "This is My people", and each one will say, 'The Lord is my God' - **Zechariah 13:9**

CHARACTERISTICS OF LACK OF MATURITY

- Disunity of the faith and strife among believers -Ephesians 4:14-15.
- Lack of knowledge of the Son of God and a weak biblical foundation.
- Being tossed to and fro and carried about with every wind of doctrine due to the absence of all 5 – fold ministries in the Church.
- Believers who apply philosophy, traditions of men and the basic principles of this world to explain the scriptures and live like a Christian will never be able to be established in faith and built up in Christ - Colossians 2:6-8.
- Neglecting the application of spiritual gifts, slacking in meditating, teaching, studying and exhorting in God's word - Colossians 1:26-28.
- Lack of good conduct - 1 Timothy 4:12-15.
- Constantly being spoon-fed with the milk of the word and being unskilled in the word of righteousness after many years of being born again.
- Believers with character defects like hypocrisy, malice, envy and all evil speaking - 1 Peter 2:1.
- Being involved in idolatry, sexual immorality, lusting after evil things, testing the Lord and constantly complaining/grumbling due to a bit of

hardship - 1 Corinthians 10:6-11.
- Always seeking to take revenge due to bitterness and unforgiveness - 1 Peter 3:9.

QUESTIONS TO PROVE YOUR MATURITY

- How do you react when the Lord is testing your faith through difficulties?
- What comments do you make while going through trials of lack, pain, sorrow or financial difficulties?
- How do you handle the anointing of God? Do you take the glory due to God for yourself when you perform working miracles, signs and wonders in the name of Jesus?
- How do you handle verbal attacks and criticism from both believers and unbelievers?
- Do you forgive those who hurt you easily?
- Do you apply patience and perseverance during trials, testings and persecutions?
- Are you perfected in love? Do you fear men and constantly seek their approval at the expense of your relationship with the Lord?
- Are you envious of your brethren's anointing while they exercise the gifts of the Holy Spirit?
- Do you get jealous when other ministries are successful?
- Are you still involved in disunity, dissension and discord among brethren, by spreading lies, half-truths and rumors?

QUESTIONS

Read the scripture on how to experience the full assurance of salvation and factors that can hinder this experience then answer the following questions.
- What is the assurance of hope?
- How do you experience this assurance?

- Who makes this assurance possible? List about 5 factors that could hinder you from experiencing the full assurance of salvation?
- How can grieving the Holy Spirit hinder you from experiencing the assurance of salvation? Read Colossians 2:2-3 and fill in the following gap: "that their hearts may be -------------- being knit together in --------------- and attaining to all riches of the full assurance --------------, to the knowledge of the ----------- of God, both of the Father and of Christ"
- Explain how being unequally yoked with unbelievers can hinder you from experiencing the full assurance of salvation?

CHAPTER 12

DAILY PRAYERS FOR NEW BELIEVERS

In the following exposition of these scriptures, it would be quite evident that these powerful scriptures are also essential prayers that can be prayed daily for spiritual growth and other blessings. However, it is as important for intercessors to pray for new believers (to prevent backsliding) as it is for them to pray for their own spiritual well being.

THE SCRIPTURAL VERSES

"Therefore, I also, after I heard of your faith in the Lord Jesus and your love for all the saints, do not cease to give thanks for you, making mention of you in my prayers:
That the God of our Lord Jesus Christ, the father of glory, may give to you the spirit of wisdom and

revelation (the disclosure of knowledge to humankind by a divine or supernatural agency) in the knowledge of Him. The eyes of your understanding being enlightened (to give spiritual insight to a person) ; that you may know what is the hope of His calling, what are the riches of the glory of His inheritance (property, wealth, resources that you inherit or received as an heir from ancestors or parents) in the saints, and what is the exceeding greatness of His power toward us who believe, according to the working of His mighty power which He worked in Christ when He raised Him from the dead and seated Him at His right hand in the heavenly places far above all principality and power and might and dominion, and every name that is named, not only in this age, but also in that which is to come." - **Ephesians 1:15-21.**

THE SCRIPTURAL PRAYERS FOR
Ephesians 1:15-21

Dear Heavenly Father, God of our Lord Jesus Christ, the glorious Father, I pray that you give me the spirit of wisdom (ability to rightfully apply knowledge) and revelation (ability to see hidden spiritual things) so that I may know you better. I also pray that the eyes of my heart are enlightened (to be illuminated by the Holy Spirit) so that I may know the hope to which you have called me, the riches of your glorious inheritance in us as saints, and your incomparable great power (resurrection power) given to all who believe in Jesus Christ which is like the working of mighty strength that was in Christ Jesus when you raised Him from the dead and seated Him at your right hand in the heavenly realms; far above all rulers and authority, power and dominion....

THE OUTCOME AND BLESSINGS OF PRAYING BIBLICAL PRAYERS

The exposition of these verses will help new believers to have a deeper understanding of the awesome power available in praying these prayers. It will help to build up your faith in God and His words and give you the assurance of not praying **amiss(**-prayers that are not in line with the will of God); hence, are not answered.

It enables you to see the efficacy of these prayers because they are prayed according to the will of God and will always be answered by God.

As you pray these prayers from **Ephesians 1:15-21** regularly, you will begin to experience a supernatural attestation of God's word and measures of the wisdom and revelation of God will be released into your spirit (inner being) that will enable you to have a deeper walk with the Lord. Then the Holy Spirit will begin to reveal the call of God on your life (divine assignment –the purpose of God, the reason He brought you to this earth). Your inheritance as a believer will also be revealed to you and the power that raised Jesus from the dead will begin to work in you. Finally, you will receive revelation of who you are in Christ Jesus.

THE SCRIPTURAL VERSES

*"I pray that out of his glorious riches He may strengthen you with power through His Spirit in your inner being, so that Christ may dwell in your hearts through faith. And I pray that you, being rooted and established (to achieve permanent acceptance for a custom, **belief** or practice) in love,*

> *may have power, together with all the saints, to grasp how wide and long and high and deep is the love of Christ, and to know this love that surpasses knowledge – that you may be filled to the measure of all the fullness of God. Now to him who is able to do immeasurably more than all we ask or imagine, according to His power that is at work within us, to Him be glory in the Church and in Christ Jesus throughout all generations, forever and ever! Amen."* **Ephesians 3:16-21**

THE SCRIPTURAL PRAYERS FOR
Ephesians 3:16-21

Dear Heavenly Father, in the name of Jesus I pray that you strengthen me with power, out of your glorious riches, in my inner being, so that Christ may dwell in my heart through faith. I also pray that I, being rooted and established in love, may have power together with my brethren, to grasp how wide, how long, how high, how deep is the love of Christ and that I may know this love which surpasses knowledge. I pray that I may be filled to the measure of all the fullness of God. Now, to you O Lord, who is able to do immeasurably more than I ask or imagine, according to your power that is at work in me, to you be glory in the Church and in Christ Jesus through all generations forever and ever! Amen.

THE OUTCOME AND BLESSINGS OF PRAYING BIBLICAL PRAYERS

The exposition of these verses helps the new Believers to have deeper understanding of the awesome power available in praying these prayers. It helps to build up your faith in God and His words with the assurance that you are not praying **amiss** - prayers that are not in line with the will of God; hence they are not answered.

It enables you to see the efficacy (something proved to be real and powerful)of these prayers as they are prayed according to the will of God and with guarantee of answers from God.

Ephesians 3:16-21 proves that a measure of divine strength is released into your inner being to strengthen you when you feel weak, tired or under any form of oppression. It also allows Jesus (and all His attributes in the bible) to dwell in your heart through faith.

Additionally, it makes you rooted and established in the love of Jesus Christ with the divine ability to grasp the width, height, length and depth of the love of Christ which surpasses all knowledge. This type of love is different from the love for a spouse, our parents or any type of love you have ever experienced on earth. It is the purest kind of love and it is unconditional(no strings attached). 1st John 3:1 gives us a brief description of this type of love;

> *"how great is the love the Father has lavished on us,*
> *that we should be called the children of God".*

It can only be grasped and understood through the Holy Spirit who will also fill you with a measure of all the fullness of God and you will have the ability to possess all the attributes of Jesus, which includes: His character(love, peace, humility, servanthood, patience, self-control, integrity) power, grace, anointing and holiness. The Holy Spirit will also give you the ability to do greater works than Jesus as He promised in John 14:12, work miracles, signs and wonders, decree a word and see manifestations, raise the dead, love your enemies and pray for those who are persecuting you.

THE SCRIPTURAL VERSES

*"For this reason, since the day we heard about you (being newly born again) emphasis mine, we have not stopped praying (interceding) for you; and asking **God to fill you with the knowledge of His will through all spiritual wisdom and understanding.** And we pray this in order that you may **live a life worthy of the Lord and may please Him in every way,** bearing **fruits (productive) in every good work (ministry), growing in the knowledge of God, being strengthened with all power according to His glorious might** so that **you may have great endurance and patience and joyfully giving thanks to the Father,** who has qualified you to share in the inheritance of the saints in the kingdom of light; for He has rescued us from the dominion of darkness and brought us into the Kingdom of the Son He loves, in whom we have redemption, the forgiveness of sins.*
- Colossians 1:9-14.

THE SCRIPTURAL PRAYERS FOR
Colossians 1:9-14

Dear heavenly Father, I pray that you fill me with the knowledge of your will (to know what He has called you to do on earth) through all spiritual wisdom (the divine ability to properly apply knowledge) and understanding. And I pray this so that I may live a life worthy of the Lord, please you in every way and continue to bear fruit (be productive) in every good work (in ministry & generally in life). I also pray that I may continue to grow (spiritual growth with the goal of reaching spiritual maturity) in the knowledge of you O Lord. I pray that I may be strengthened with all power according to your glorious might so that I may have great endurance, patience, joy and always give thanks to you, O God, I thank you for counting me worthy to share in the inheritance of the saints in the kingdom of Light. I also thank you for rescuing me from the kingdom of darkness and bringing me into the kingdom of the Son that you love; and in Him (Jesus) my sins are forgiven and I am redeemed with His precious blood. In Jesus' name. Amen.

OUTCOME AND BLESSINGS OF PRAYING BIBLICAL PRAYERS

Exposition of these verses helps the new Believers to have deeper understanding of the awesome power available in praying these prayers.
It helps to build up your faith in God and His words with the assurance that you are not praying **amiss - prayers** that are not in line with the will of God; hence they are not answered.

It enables you to see the efficacy of these prayers as they are prayed according to the will of God and with guarantee of answers from God.

Colossians 1:9-14 affirms that praying these prayers regularly will fill you with the knowledge of God's will, spiritual wisdom and understanding. Then a measure of God's wisdom will be released into your inner being (heart) with the ability to understand the will of God for your life, this includes: God's promise to prosper you and bring you to an expected end (prosperity of the spirit, soul and body) as promised in Jeremiah 29:11, to protect you from the hands of satan and keep you in divine health and strength.

The word of God also declares that it is not His will for anyone to perish, but come to repentance; in other words, whenever you sin against

Him, you simply need to repent and the joy of salvation will be restored to you. Besides, He will give you grace to live a life worthy of Him and the ability to please Him through faith by meditating on His word, thanking, praising, worshipping and adoring Him daily with reverence.

He will also give you the grace to walk with the Holy Spirit to receive direction, guidance and to obey i.e. His instructions and walking closely with the Holy Spirit will make you fruitful (being productive) in every good work (the specific divine assignment given to you). Finally, a measure of divine strength will be released to you for endurance, patience, joy and a heart of gratitude to the Lord.

He will also give you the grace to walk with the Holy Spirit to receive direction, guidance and to obey i.e. His instructions and walking closely with the Holy Spirit will make you fruitful (being productive) in every good work (the specific divine assignment given to you). Finally, a measure of divine strength will be released to you for endurance, patience, joy and a heart of gratitude to the Lord.

WORDSEARCH
THE WORD OF GOD

L	P	S	Y	B	O	G	E	L	A	M	P
I	O	T	Z	I	Z	P	R	O	L	E	G
V	W	R	S	B	L	L	R	O	G	N	O
I	E	E	I	L	A	I	O	K	I	L	L
N	R	N	L	W	S	F	R	T	J	K	D
G	F	G	V	E	O	E	A	H	L	D	E
B	U	T	E	O	Y	T	E	I	A	C	J
A	L	H	R	E	I	Q	M	D	D	G	P
O	K	P	N	D	E	C	A	N	R	U	F
L	E	O	E	B	G	N	I	L	A	E	H
R	H	M	S	E	E	M	I	R	R	O	R

1. One purpose of the word of God is? (2nd Timothy 3:16)
2. You let the word of God dwell richly in you, by doing this (Colossians 3:16)
3. In the beginning was the word and the word was with God and the word was God. Who is the word of God? (Genesis 1:3 & John 1:1-14)
4. The word of God is like a ------------- (Psalm 119:105)
5. The word of God is like ---------------- (Proverbs 25:12)

198 *Elementary Principles of Christ*

6. The word of God is sweeter than this (Psalm 119:103)
7. This is the definition of the word of God. It is ------- and ------------ (Hebrews 4:12)
8. The word of God gives this to believers (Psalm 119:50)
9. The word of God is likened to this when planted (Luke 18:11)
10. The word of God is settled forever in this place
11. Lord, open my eyes that I may ---- wondrous things from your law (Psalm 119:18)
12. Believers receive this from the word of God (Psalm 119:107)
13. "This book of the -------- shall not depart from your mouth" Joshua 1:8
14. This is one of the promises of God in His word
15. The word of the Lord are pure words, like ------ tried in the --------of the earth, purifies seven times (Psalm 12:6)
16. God promised to do this to anyone who takes His word seriously (Isaiah 66:2(a)
17. The word of God is like a ------------ James 1:23
18. The word of God is like ------------- I Peter 2:2
19. The word of God is without this ………… (Proverbs 30:5-6)

Answers to the word search - The word of God
1. Reproof   2. Meditating 3. Jesus 4. Lamp 5. Gold 6. Honey 7. Living, Powerful 8. Life 9. Seed 10. Heaven 11. See 12. Strength 13. Law 14. Healing 15. Silver, Furnace 16. Look 17. Mirror 18. Milk 19. Error

WORDSEARCH

ELEMENTARY PRINCIPLES OF CHRIST

F	G	R	A	C	E	L	I	F	E
A	C	L	J	E	W	N	N	B	T
I	R	I	A	T	M	E	C	C	I
T	O	N	E	E	R	A	E	R	R
H	W	E	D	D	E	R	D	E	I
E	N	N	L	S	R	D	O	A	P
L	O	I	U	U	J	E	R	T	S
C	H	S	S	P	P	A	C	I	Y
C	E	E	P	E	N	T	A	O	L
J	R	L	O	V	E	H	S	N	O
R	I	N	H	E	R	I	T	E	H

1. This person died for the sins of all human race
2. To bring a dead person to life is to do this
3. God gave the right to all who accept Jesus to become ------------- of God
4. It is by this you have been saved ....

5. This person is the promised Helper to all believers on earth
6. God demonstrated this to all people ....
7. He who overcomes will ----------------- all this (Revelation 21:7)
8. If anyone is in Christ Jesus, He is a new ...., the old has gone and the new has come (2nd Corinthians 5:17)
9. This is what would be done to those who reject Jesus Christ on earth
10. Apostle Peter raised this woman from death to life..................
11. Jesus has power over this (Hebrews 2:14)......................
12. Without this it is impossible to please God! ....
13. This is one of the material rewards Jesus promised to anyone who endured hardship, fulfilled his ministry on earth and made it to heaven

Answers to the word search - The Elementary Principles Of Christ
1. Jesus 2.Resurrect 3.Children 4.Grace 5.HolySpirit 6.Love 7.Inherit 8.Creation 9.Condemned 10.Dorcas 11. Death 12. Faith 13. Crown

Answers to the word search - The word of God
1. Reproof 2. Meditating 3.Jesus 4.Lamp 5.Gold 6. Honey 7. Living, Powerful 8.Life 9.Seed 10.Heaven 11.See 12.Strength 13.Law 14.Healing 15. Silver, Furnace 16.Look 17.Mirror 18.Milk 19.Error

BIBLIOGRAPHY

Conner Kevin J © The Foundations of Christian Doctrine. Sovereign World International. Kent. England. 1980.

Prince, Derek © Foundation For Righteous Living. Derek Prince Ministries. UK. 1993.

Strong James, LLD., S.T.D © STRONG'S CONCORDANCE OF THE BIBLE

New Kings James Version Bible © 1978 New Spirit Filled Life Bible, Nelson.

Holy Bible, New International Version (NIV) © 1973, 1978, 1984 by International Bible Society.

God's Promises For Today's Believers, Published by Whitaker House, 1997, New Kensington, PA 15068.

PRAYER OF SALVATION

If you would like to accept the Lord Jesus as your Savior and Lord, simply pray the following prayer in faith.

Heavenly Father, I come to you in the name of Jesus. I acknowledge that I am a sinner, I ask for your forgiveness. Your word says, "Whosoever shall call on the name of the Lord shall be saved" (Acts 2:21). Lord Jesus, come into my heart, and be the Lord and Savior over my life. Romans 10:9-10 says: "If you confess with your mouth the Lord Jesus and believe in your heart that God has raised Him from the dead, you will be saved."
I confess that Jesus is Lord, and I believe in my heart that God raised Him from the dead.
Your word also says, "If you then being evil know how to give good gifts to your children, how much more will your heavenly Father give the Holy Spirit to those who ask Him."
I also ask you to fill me with your Holy Spirit with the evidence of speaking in tongues as you give me utterance according to your promise in Acts 2:4.
I thank you Lord Jesus for saving me and for filling me with your Holy Spirit. Thank you that I am born-again.

If you have prayed this prayer, please write to us and let us know your decision.